FARMFIELDS TO AIRFIELDS

FARMFIELDS TO AIRFIELDS

A LIFE'S JOURNEY FROM WEST WALES TO NORFOLK
(CAEAU Y FFERM I'R MAESAWRENAU)

WILLIAM WYNDHAM LEWIS

AN AUTOBIOGRAPHY

1918 -

COPYRIGHT

While I have taken advantage of a minimum amount of material which could be considered to be copyright, serious efforts have been made to obtain permission from holders to do so.
There are indications on some material, suggesting that copyright dates have expired.

If it is considered that there are, in this material, circumstances where copyright has been breached then the writer sincerely apologises to those concerned.

This book of my history was not originally intended for public reading or for general distribution. However, as it has now, inadvertently, found its way into wider circles, it is hoped that the contents will not cause offence or embarrassment to the many friends and associates that I lived, worked and laughed with many years ago.

Wyndham

ISBN: 0-9545591-0-X
Published by Molwyn Books
Printed by The Lanceni Press, Fakenham, Norfolk

Ploughing and mowing pictured by kind permission of J. Salmon Ltd.
Drawing of Elim Chapel by J W Bamford

1st Edition produced in 1991
2nd Edition produced in 2001
3rd Edition produced in 2002
4th Edition produced in 2003 (Revised)

FOREWORD

The early part of this book provides a rare insight into a period of recent history, that sees the advent of mechanized farming replacing manual and horse drawn equipment. That in itself should command it's reading, but it is the personal and intimate nature of the descriptions of what it was really like to live 'close to nature', and be totally involved in scraping a living from agriculture in a small geographical area of South West Wales.

As someone who has lived in St. Clears for a long time, I was absolutely fascinated by the references to actual farms and place names in my area. I know that the present population of this part of Wales will be equally entranced by these accounts of life not so distant, and that it occurred very near.

It begins like a West Walian's 'Cider With Rosie', and continues like a Welsh 'Precious Bane'. I can commend it equally with these great accounts of country living to locals and visitors alike.

It had me rushing to my map to try and locate each farm, and was continually amazed at the human endeavor involved in just living here, around St. Clears, at that time.

DAVID PETERSON
Broadcaster and Artist
Chairman of A.C.T. Local Enterprise Agency for
SW Carmarthenshire.

INTRODUCTION

Great Newton Farm lies deep in the heart of the beautiful countryside of South West Carmarthenshire, near the border with Pembrokeshire. I visited this historic farm for the first time in 2000 at the kind invitation of its owner Geoff Evans. During my visit Geoff introduced me to his two sons Lloyd and Bobby who help him in managing the farm. Bobby, the younger son has a particular interest in historical matters and because of this he showed me a book that he had been given by a visitor to the farm. The author of this book, Wyndham Lewis had worked at Great Newton before the war and there were a number of references to the Farm in the book. Bobby very kindly offered to lend me the book and I took it home with me to read.

That evening as I began to read the book I soon realised that it contained marvellous descriptions of life on farms in this corner of Wales at a time when the centuries old traditional farming methods still existed and had yet to be replaced by the new intensive agricultural practices introduced during the war that changed farming methods beyond recognition. I became so engrossed and fascinated by the book that I could not put it down until I had finished reading it. By this time I felt that I must find out more about the author and whether he was still alive and living locally. My enquiries revealed that Wyndham Lewis, the author, was in his eighties and living in Norfolk. I was fortunate enough to obtain his address and telephone number through members of his family still living locally, which enabled me subsequently to make contact with him. When I did this he explained that the purpose of the book was to put his life on record for his own family, particularly his wife and daughters in Norfolk. Accordingly he had a dozen copies made for his family and it was one of those copies that found its way to Bobby Evans at Great Newton farm.

Having been captivated and fascinated by his account of life first as a farm worker then with The Royal Air Force and finally with the Construction Industry, I felt that his career - particularly his early years in farming would be of great interest to many people outside that of his immediate family and friends. I am delighted therefore that Wyndham has agreed to bring out this new edition of his memoirs and making it available to a wider audience.

I hope that my enjoyment of the book will now be shared by many other people and that they will find this account of his career equally interesting and be fascinated by a successful and varied career which has led him from the pre war world of farming in Wales to retirement in the opposite side of the country in East Anglia.

NOEL KING
Chairman, 'Friends of the Carmarthenshire Archives'
MAY 2003

FARMFIELDS TO AIRFIELDS
A LIFE'S JOURNEY FROM WEST WALES TO NORFOLK
(CAEAU Y FFERM I'R MAESAWRENAU)

INDEX **PAGE NO**

ACKNOWLEDGEMENTS

This autobiography would not be complete if I did not mention the help I have received from my family and friends in its final preparation. My wife Mollie deserves special mention, for her most valuable effort in the typing and editing of the material throughout the various stages to the final production. Credit is also due to my daughter Mandy who was responsible for the original print out.

My thanks to Mr John Boucher (my nephew) and Mr Bobby Evans of Great Newton, who deserve a mention for their original involvement in the 'airing' of the book. A special mention is due to Noel King who has been mainly responsible for bringing the book to the public notice.

Thanks to Dr. Trevor Jones, St. Clears, Mr David Howells, Llanddowror and Mr Dewi Thomas of Carmarthen Library for their help encouragement and advice. Thanks also to Mr Geoffrey Watts for providing the appropriate title for the book.

Special thanks to Mr David Petersen and again to Mr Noel King of Laugharne who have registered their prominence in writing the foreword and introduction respectively.

LIFETIME CALENDAR

YEAR	AGE	DETAIL
1918	*-*	*Born at Penrallt, Llanddowror*
1919	*1*	*Bronhaul, Laugharne*
1920	*2*	
1921	*3*	
1922	*4*	
1923	*5*	
1924	*6*	*Broadmoor, St Clears*
1925	*7*	
1926	*8*	
1927	*9*	
1928	*10*	
1929	*11*	
1930	*12*	
1931	*13*	*Cwrt-y-Bedw, Llangynog*
1932	*14*	*Castell Farm, Llangynog*
1933	*15*	*Frongelly, Bronwydd*
1934	*16*	
1935	*17*	
1936	*18*	*Moor Farm, St Clears*
1937	*19*	
1938	*20*	*Great Newton, Llanddowror*
1939	*21*	
1940	*22*	
1941	*23*	*Great Newton*
1942	*24*	*Penarth - Padgate - Blackpool*
1943	*25*	*RAF Mill Green, Hatfield*
1944	*26*	*Elstead - Normandy - France*
		Belgium - Holland
1945	*27*	*Germany - Singapore*
1946	*28*	*Bron-y-Glyn*
1947	*29*	*Mother died*

continued/

1949	*31*	*Rejoined RAF*	
		Church Lawford	*Corporal*
1950	*32*	*RAF Germany*	
1951	*33*	*Sundern – Rinteln*	*Sergeant*
1952	*34*	*RAF Wildenrath*	*Father died*
1953	*35*	*RAF Bruggen*	*F/Sergeant*
1954	*36*	*From Germany*	*Warrant Officer*
1955	*37*	*RAF Wellesbourne UK*	
1956	*38*	*Plant Training School*	*Married*
1957	*39*		*Michelle born*
1962	*44*	*Posted to Cyprus*	
1963	*45*	*Singapore – Borneo*	
		Sarawak – Kuchin – Labuan	
1964	*46*	*Singapore – Thailand*	
1965	*47*	*Returned to UK*	
1966	*48*	*Demobbed*	*Mandy born*
1967	*49*	*Bircham Newton*	
		Training Centre	*Instructor*
1970	*52*	"	*Senior Instructor*
1983	*65*	*Retired Norfolk*	

PREFACE

This story started out as some of the epic events in my life, but having started to outline these I found it difficult not to mention those around, especially brother, sister, mother, father; then there are friends, school mates and neighbours. The longer the story then the more that are involved.

So what started out as a personal history has I'm afraid developed into a rather wider circle of events, some of which may not seem to involve me too closely but I can assure your that if I can still remember them, they are worth mentioning. I have realised at the time of writing that some of these may not be of much interest to readers - but there you are - there are pages in most books that can be skipped.

My biggest problem in writing this was how to give a true account of your own experiences and these of course would be your best, without being said to be boasting or bragging - difficult!

So I have tried to tell the truth though this may sound a bit tame at times, it is intended to also highlight the other more favourable occasions.

GAIR BACH YN NGHYMRAUG

I POB UN SYDD YN MYNED I DDARLLEN HWN YR WYF YN DWEUD WRTHINT YR WYF FI WEDI YSCRAFENI YR HANES YMA YN OL FY NGOF GORAU AM YR PRID HYNU.

OS YDYCH CHWI YN GWYBOD AM YR AMSER AR BOBL YMA FALLE BOD EICH COF CHWI YN WAHANIAITH - ANGHOFIWCH - DARLLENWCH A GOBEITHIO GALLWCH MYWNHAU YR HANES HWN.

WYNDHAM

Translation of Welsh above:-

A LITTLE WORD IN WELSH

TO EVERYONE THAT INTENDS TO READ THIS I WOULD SAY TO THEM I HAVE WRITTEN THIS HISTORY ACCORDING TO MY BEST MEMORIES OF THAT PERIOD.

IF YOU ARE FAMILIAR WITH THIS TIME AND THE PEOPLE MAYBE YOUR MEMORIES ARE DIFFERENT - FORGET - READ - AND I HOPE THAT YOU WILL ENJOY THIS BIT OF MY HISTORY:

WYNDHAM

LITTLE MEMORIES

I CAN WELL REMEMBER
THE FARM WHERE I WAS BORN
WITH MANY KINDS OF ANIMALS
THE COCK THAT CROWED AT DAWN.

I HAVE NOT FORGOTTEN
THE YELLOW FRONTED FARMHOUSE
AND THE ROOM WHERE WE
AS CHILDREN SLEPT

AND THEN DOWNSTAIRS THE DAIRY
WHERE THE MILK AND BUTTER'S KEPT.

I REMEMBER YET THE SUMMER DAYS
WHEN WE ALL WENT OUT TO PLAY,

ESPECIALLY AT HARVEST TIME,
AND THE CARS WE MADE OF HAY.

WE WERE JUST AS LITTLE CHILDREN
IN AMONG'ST IT ALL

AT THAT VERY TENDER AGE WHEN
EVERYTHING LOOKED TALL.

I REMEMBER YET THE CUCKOO THAT CAME
IN SPRINGTIME TO UTTER ITS STRANGE SOUND

I REMEMBER - MOTHER TOLD US IT WAS
THE STRANGEST BIRD AROUND.

I REMEMBER TOO THE PEACEFUL DAYS
WHEN WE PLAYED IN SECRET PLACES,

WHEN THE ONLY SOUND EVER HEARD WAS FROM
IMAGINARY PEOPLE WITH IMAGINARY FACES.

THEN CAME THE COLD WINTER NIGHTS WITH THE
OIL LAMPS AND THE CANDLES TO LIGHT US UP TO BED,

WITH THE REMAINS OF THAT OLD LOG FIRE
WITH THE EMBERS STILL BURNING RED.

I REMEMBER THE WARM SUMMER DAYS
THAT NOW SEEM SO FAR AWAY

AND YET IN OUR CHILDISH MINDS
COULD RETURN MAYBE ANY DAY.

THERE ARE LOTS OF LITTLE MEMORIES IN LIFE
FROM THE TIME WHEN WE WERE SMALL

AND THE MEMORIES OF OUR CHILDHOOD
ARE THE STRONGEST OF THEM ALL.

<u>**SECTION I**</u>

CHAPTER I

MY CHILDHOOD

My father and mother were both born within half a mile of each other, near the village of Llanddowror in the county of Carmarthen in South Wales - father in a place called The Bont - when translated means The Bridge, and mother a little further along the road in a thatched cottage called Bronhaul.

They both attended the same school in the village and it seems they were childhood sweethearts. This may sound rather romantic but considering that they did not get married until mother was about twenty-eight years old - they were apparently too busy earning their own livings - father as a farm worker and mother as a dressmaker.

As was customary in those days, life centred around the village and in particular the Chapel. This was to play an important part in father's life until the end of his days and to a lesser extent to us as his children.

After their marriage they were to start their married life in The Bont, in other words father's home and it was here that Ben my older brother (who was incidentally eleven years older than me) was born and started school while they were still there.

Father who was a farm worker, had worked for eleven years in a farm called Parce. It was customery to reward workers for long and loyal service. If an employee worked for the same employer (farmer) for seven years or more, it seems that he would be entitled to a young heifer or the equivilent in moneys. I am not sure that this custom was honoured in all cases or even in my father's case. Father was now working in Cwmbrwyn. He had I believe worked in Trecoed.

Cwmbrwyn was about a mile from his home. Now that he was a married man with a family he was given the opportunity of moving to a small holding called Penyrallt near to his workplace. This then was where my sister Betty and I were born as I was not much more than one year old when we left Penyrallt. I have no memories but I was to be told a tale involving Ben and Betty - Ben who must have been twelve years old and Betty two or three. It seems that Ben was pushing Betty in a little cart and as our house was on top of a steep hill, he apparently pushed the cart down the field and over a very steep drop onto the road - she must have survived without injury.

Somewhere around this time we moved from Penyrallt to a place called Bronhaul - this was a small farm some five miles as the crow flies - cross country. This was a coincidence as mother's original home was the same name but no connection. Both my sisters, Mary and Audrey, were born here.

Bronhaul had a lot more land than Penyrallt but as Ben was now around school leaving age, this meant that his help at home allowed father to seek casual work elsewhere as he had done before. The earlier years at Bronhaul are not clear in my mind as I was too young to remember, but I somehow remember he did a kind of contract work - like tree felling and hay trussing. Although he spent most of this time at home he would sometimes be away for a week at a time, returning at weekends. I also remember later on father and my brother were interested in steam engine driving.

One job was driving a steam engine which towed a thrashing machine. This was I think, owned by a consortium and it was taken from farm to farm during the season to carry out the threshing of the corn. If I remember correctly father did this initially and Ben got involved later when he was old enough. The work was seasonal and was for a duration of about two months in the autumn.

The second job was also driving a steam engine but this was a steam roller owned by the County Council and the job was regular and fairly permanent. These two main jobs which continued for some years were to involve father for most of the week days and later Ben was involved with the seasonal job. Somehow or other this did leave father or Ben at home to do the farm jobs.

My own memories of this very early age are of play and certain very special occurrences - like when I chopped my sister Mary's finger with a chopper which father had left on the chopping block - he did usually put it out of our reach. I distinctly remember asking Mary "Do you want your finger chopped off?" She said "Yes" - me "Put it there" and believe it or not I got hold of the chopper with both hands and brought it down on her finger and cut it very badly. She still bears the mark even to this day.

As Mary and I were very near in age we were around and played together most of the time. I remember well both of us chasing the very young ducklings hoping to catch one each but unfortunately we only caught one and as both of us wanted it we pulled it in two pieces; how cruel we must have been - very young!

Another very vivid memory I have is of me and Mary, yes both of us again, playing around the yard - somehow I was either pushed or I fell flat on my face into the pond - the contents of which came from the cow muck heap - I remember it was green. After I was rescued by my mother and eventually cleaned up, or thought I was clean, I realised that I was chewing something and when I spat it out it turned out to be a worm.

I remember another occasion one Sunday morning in the house as nothing much happened on a Sunday. It was approaching dinner time and as a good indication mother had just made a large boiler full of 'cawl' (a mixture of boiled meat and vegetables) and had removed it from the fire – taken the lid off and placed the boiler on the kitchen floor to allow it to cool prior to being served up – usually with a big 'lletwad' which was a large wooden ladle that had a curved end to prevent it slipping into the boiler.

While all this was going on, we, as children had been playing in another room, when we decided to race or probably answer a call for dinner, chased each other into the kitchen unaware of the boiler on the floor. When we did realise, it was too late and I ended up with my boot in the boiler. I was wearing big, hobnailed boots at the time which I suppose saved me from a scalding but you can imagine the scolding I got from my mum and dad. To be fair they were really concerned that I may have been scalded but I had not. I do not remember what we had for dinner – it certainly was not cawl.

These are the kind of things one remembers I suppose, the unusual and this would include the happy memories as most of mine are of this period but as mother and father had to work hard to earn a living, I sometimes think of the worries my mum must have had. Ben my brother was about sixteen years old and was able to do a fair share of the work while father was away.

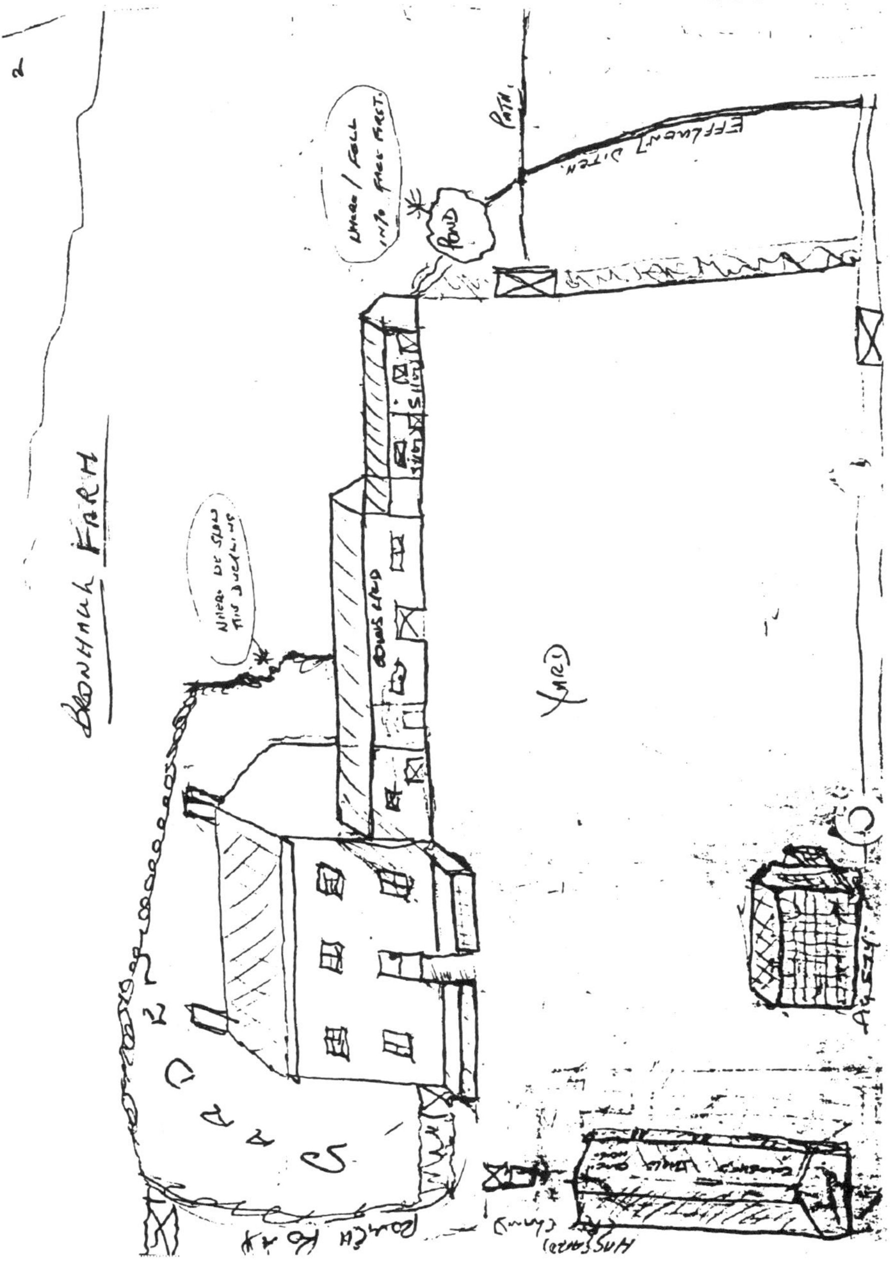
FARM
POND
YARD
PATH

I remember one day while my mother was out feeding the animals - probably the pigs - she had left the house door open when she went out and the next thing I remember was my mum shouting something and I found out that the horse that had been in the yard had decided to have a look into our kitchen. Can you imagine a horse turning around in the kitchen - well that is what it did do and it came out again.

It was customary in those days for farmers to help each other on occasions such as haymaking, potato planting etc. It was on one of these 'chores' - potatoes I think - that Ben had gone to help Mr Lewis - Cresswell Farm, our neighbour with and I suppose several other people helped as well. One of these 'others' a Mr Thomas, an older man, asked Ben if he could borrow his double barrelled gun to shoot crows. They had an understanding that when he finished with it, he would leave it in the hedge where Ben could pick it up on his way home. Ben being young and maybe not as careful as he should have been - went to collect the gun - he grabbed it by the barrel and when he pulled it out, the trigger caught in some twigs and as the old man had not bothered to unload it, the gun fired and Ben was shot in the arm. It was a serious accident and it was to leave his hand deformed for the rest of his life. He was needless to say, in hospital for a long time, months I think. For me and my sisters it must have seemed ages as we at that age were very shy and hardly remembered Ben when he came out of hospital.

I remember mother saying that when Ben eventually came home he still had the muck on his hand that he had when he was admitted as it was the practice in those days not to wash wounds. However, Ben was soon to recover to take his place in the working order and once more he would help mother during father's absence in the week until father returned at the weekend.

There is one thing that I have not mentioned or should I say that I have forgotten to mention. How could I, even at five years old forget when I started smoking - yes a pipe. I somehow got hold of a stem of father's old pipe (real rich it was) I went out to walk around the field with this in my mouth and hands in my little trouser pockets - like father I suppose! I had not gone far before I got that horrible giddy feeling when the whole world started spinning and the field seemed to come up to meet me. I threw away the pipe but it was too late. When I arrived back my mother said I looked green and after telling her the reason mother put me to lie down on the couch until I was able to catch up with the world.

As our farm was some distance from the main road and as we had no means of transport all travelling had to be done by 'shank's pony' walking on a very rough cart track on an adjoining farmer's land.

In addition to the farm land we had a 'share' some distance away. This was part of a large area of land owned by the council rented in the form of shares to individual farmers. All this land was open unfenced and was used entirely for the growing of crops including hay which was harvested and stored in ricks until it was required for fodder for the cattle in the winter. I remember my mother telling me that during one winter my brother Ben had carried a daily 'quota' of this hay until he had carried the whole rick which must have been five or six tons, over a distance of one and half to two miles. The other commodity that had to be carried was all the drinking water - this came from Cresswell Farm over two fields away.

Among'st the daily visitors to our isolated house was of course, the postman - strangely enough we seem to have had the same one for years. His job was a 'taxing one' as he was involved in so much travel to deliver, maybe one unimportant letter – granted in those days we did not have much 'junk mail'.

His route was the same every day. I suppose pathways and right-of-way was a lot simpler in those days and the postman would naturally choose the shortest and most convenient way to and from each dwelling. I remember from my young days that the postman was assessed once each year or so. For what ever reason I do not know but I do remember the postman briefing us all prior to this occasion. I think now with hindsight the purpose was twofold – to assess the time taken and the degree of difficulty of the travel. This I suppose would affect his pay. For obvious purposes we were, it seems, to describe his route, some of which was nigh impassable through deep muddy gateways, which of course he never did use. The assessor would accompany the postman once a year – poor man – surely it was he that would most likely need a pay rise?

Walking in those days was fairly normal way of getting around and considering that the nearest village - St Clears - was some three or four miles away some considerable time had to be spent in fetching and carrying the necessities of life.

One day I remember, father had to go to the station to collect a parcel which turned out to be a big family bible. For some reason which escapes me now I along with my sisters waited patiently by the side of the path along which my father would return. I must have fallen asleep because when I woke up I was alone and father had returned and my sisters had gone along home with him. Needless to say I could not have come to any harm but I was not pleased.

Sometime before the end of our five years at Bronhaul we had a pony and I have vivid memories of this pony grazing in a field along with the cows and as there was a gap in the hedge which separated it from the adjoining hayfield, I was given the job of sitting in the gap to prevent the pony going into the hay until my father returned from St Clears and this was some considerable time. I am glad to say that I did not go to sleep on this occasion.

At this tender age I remember asking my mother which day was my growing up day! This is the time when events however simple are exciting and seem to be important. I have vivid memories of making a nest for a hen to lay in out of hay -this was in a stall in the stable. I was very excited the next day when I discovered that a hen had indeed laid an egg in it.

Haymaking was always a very exciting time - this was I suppose the fact that it was always associated with warm sunny days and often what we children considered a tea party in the field with hot freshly baked 'picks'. These were currant buns and were of course teatime food for the people working with the hay. Most farmers brewed beer for haymaking time. One occasion which must have made some impression on my little mind was during haymaking; my brother Ben was working the hay with Ivor a lad of the same age, who was a cousin of ours from Cardiff. He came in the summer time for a holiday. He was on this occasion supposedly helping Ben but it seemed that Ivor, in spite of the fact that he was a town lad, was trying to advise Ben regarding the hay. Ben resented this and somehow an argument ensued during which Ivor threatened to get the gun and shoot Ben - this of course was only meant to frighten him but it was in very bad taste after Ben's previous accident with a gun. My memories of this are of Ben sending me to tell mother to hide the gun (happy days eh!) Father during this time was working on the roller but he would come home for occasions like harvesting. This often started later in the day as it required 'to make' during the day.

In nineteen twenty four after five years at Bronhaul father negotiated an agreement for another neighbouring farm called Broadmoor and was situated (in country language) three fields away. I can well remember the time we moved; everything had to be taken across the fields to Broadmoor. I helped to drive the cows over - how much help I was at five years old? You can guess! At least I did walk all the way and what was important - I went with the men. I cannot remember being sorry to be leaving the only home I had ever known. I suppose that this was overshadowed by the exitement of going to a new place.

I have already said that Broadmoor was a bigger farm and this was the reason for the move and although I was only five years old I was in my way of thinking also big! This attitude was to prove very important in the immediate future as in the years from seven to ten I seemed to have been cast in a mould which shaped my early life and had an effect on the rest of my life.

My sisters and I lived in Broadmoor and there was no reason to go anywhere at all and apart from school which came to me a little later this was our world - a complete Welsh one. I cannot recollect speaking English much before school days. Incidentally this was considered to be one of the added problems of going to school but I think now that children pick up this kind of thing quickly from each other. Thinking back to those tender years I came to the conclusion that these few years were the only time in my life when I had the freedom of childhood as soon, all too soon I suppose, I was to be more and more involved in helping around the farm. My involvment came very naturally to me as I was always very interested and along with this I suppose, father realised as well. He therefore encouraged me and often involved me in activities which should even at that age be considered too adult. This was often with the disappoval of my mother.

I, like other boys of my age had interest in playing, although most games were, in one way or another related to what father did. I spent a lot of my time making a small cart which consisted of a box and two wheels, one of which was damaged. This was still my major hobby, even when I started school. I remember going to the grocery shop (Miss Griffiths) and asking for a tea chest for my cart, the cost of this was sixpence. The grocer lady was to ask my father to bring it home during his milk run and of course pay the sixpence. Father was not prepared to pay the sixpence, so I did not get my box. Sixpence in those days was a lot more than it is now. You could get a packet of Players or a pint of beer for that amount, or todays equivalent of a two and a half penny stamp which was in those days, one and a half d.

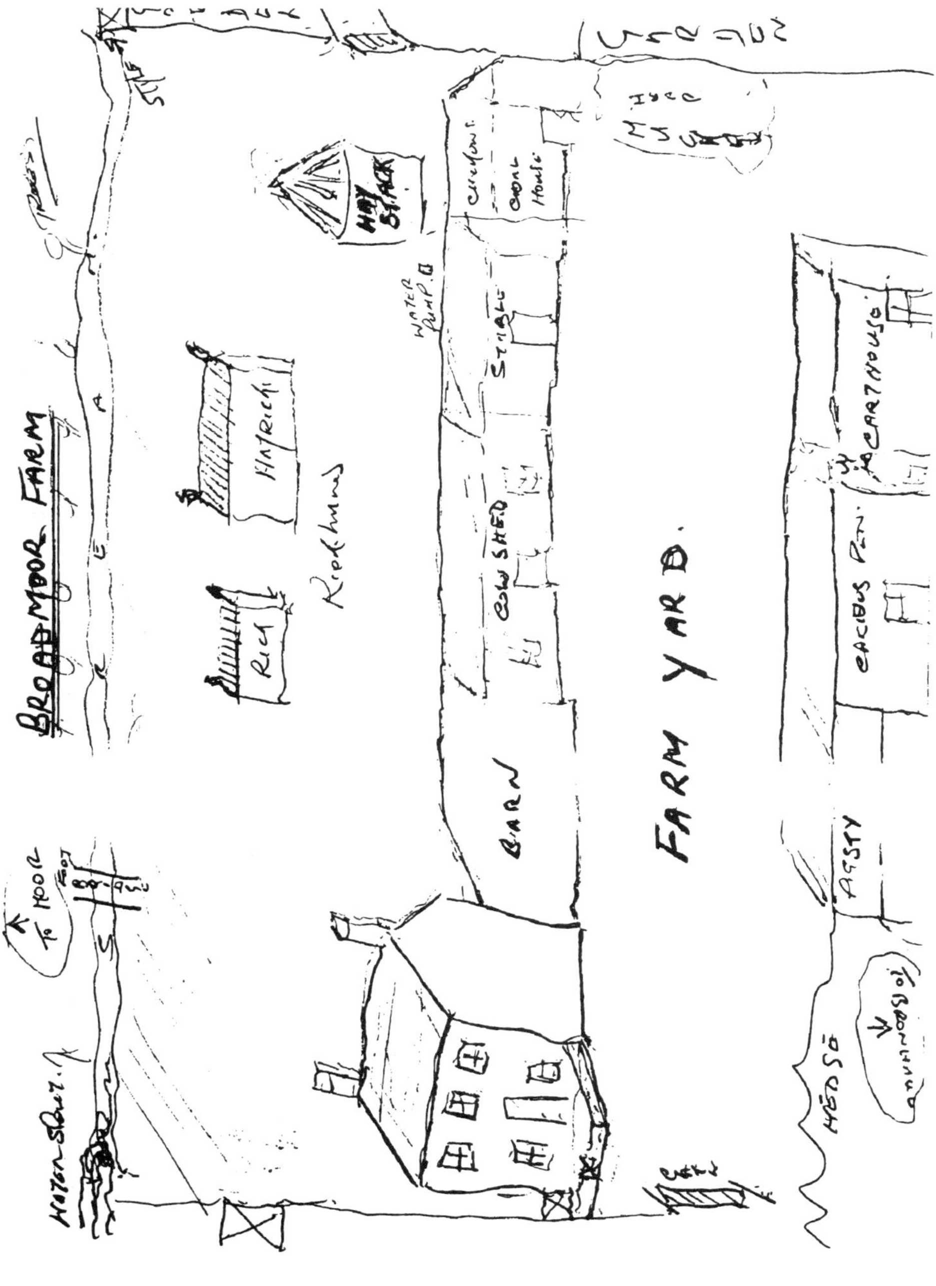
BROADMOOR FARM
FARM YARD.
BARN
COW SHED
STABLE
HAY STACK
RICK
HAYRICK
WATER PUMP
COAL HOUSE
CARTHOUSE
PIGSTY
TO MOOR

CHAPTER 11

SCHOOL DAYS

My school was the 'National School' at St Clears; it was a church school although this did not mean much to me then. Normally I would have gone to school with my sister Betty but for some reason which escapes me now I had to go on my own on the second day. I was taken down to the main road by my father at the same time as he took the milk churns. There I was to meet up with Oswald, an older boy who would take me. When we arrived at the arranged meeting place my father explained to me that we were too late as Oswald had already gone. The indication of this was a stone placed on top of the gate; this concerned me but I was told that I had to go on my own and although I cannot remember a lot about the journey of three miles - I must have got there eventually.

After this day I remember school days and the journey to and from each day became a lot easier and more fun. I eventually discovered that several other children travelled together and as some were older than me they would kind of 'look after' us. The journey was really three miles on the main road, these days I suppose it seems unreasonable to allow children as young to walk this road.

The traffic was minimal I suppose compared with later days. There were vehicles that were encountered regularly; there was for a start - a bus service - I believe it was from Laugharne to Carmarthen and it went to Pendine in the summertime. Then there was the blue lorry and the grey lorry and later the Foden steam lorry which carried stone from Coygen quarries in Laugharne. I can remember seeing, just before my school days, a steam engine towing a number of wagons again carrying stone. Cars seemed to be few and far between in those days in that particular part of the world and were used mainly for pleasure.

This then was the traffic scene and it remained so for some years. I do remember a little later another vehicle, a rather special type which appeared during the holiday period - it was a 'Charabanc' - an open topped bus - usually going to and from Pendine which was a very popular seaside place.

The horse and trap was by far the most widely used. The journey to the milk factory in the morning was a daily trip and any requirements like animal fodder, groceries etc, were usually collected then. Little did I realise then that I was destined to become part of the traffic at a very early age - this will become evident later.

The speed of the traffic in those days was slow compared with today and it was quite common practice for us to catch hold of the rear end of lorries whilst they were at their slowest going up hill and run behind. The secret was to know when to let go. You may think that this would be easy - the only way to find out would be to try it out as when you are taken along beyond your own running speed you are controlled by the hold on the lorry. We treated this as a game and the challenge was that the last one to let go was the winner. On one occasion I remember we all let go at the top of the hill - all except Mary -she carried on and while we all thought how clever she was while she went on and on - it was not until we heard her shout that we realised that she was not going voluntarily - she was being towed along. Eventually she let herself fall off and was very fortunate not to be hurt. The lorry driver would not even be aware of hangers on!

Two or three years after I started school my young life was quietly changing as my father involved me in more and more jobs - appropriate to my size, age and ability. My playtime was usually restricted to gaps in my work rather than the other way round. I was of course, proud of the fact that I was so involved in work. It made one feel big and important and sometimes very tired. Summer evenings did allow more spare time for my own interests.

TRANSPORT

I remember well the days of steam
When it featured on our roads.
The traction engine pulled its trucks
Hauling heavy loads.

With wheels made of iron,
Solid tyres tough as nails.
It looked like a locomotive
That had just come off the rails.

It could be heard approaching
As it huffed and puffed along,
Travelling very slowly –
But oh, so very strong.

But the days of steam and solid tyres
Were very soon to end,
As the advent of the petrol
Was just around the bend.

Along came the lorry
With its new pneumatic tyre
And it had a petrol engine
That did not need a fire.

Things are still progressing –
Wagons growing bigger every day,
If we think of 'artic' loaders
And 'pantecs' up so high.

We have now come full circle
With trucks just like the past,
Long – with many axles
But now – they move so fast.

I have some lovely memories of summer evenings. I remember Willy - Moor Bach -practising his mouth organ whilst out in the fields - a lovely sound.

A farm is a very big playground and we often went to different fields to explore gullies and brooks where the animals had made tracks, when they would go in the warm weather into the cool of the brook and the shade of the trees. On one such occasion I well remember Betty, Mary, Audrey and myself went roaming around such a place where we would probably play hide and seek and it was not until we arrived back home that we realised that Audrey, who was the youngest, was missing. There had been the possibility that she had arrived home on her own but she had not. This as you can imagine caused some alarm as anything could have happened amongst the pools where we had been, and as it was now late evening soon to get dark, we had to return with mother immediately to the place where we had been playing. After a little while we found Audrey fast asleep in a comfy little corner in the grass. Needless to say we were all very relieved.

We were sometimes joined in our games by Leslie, he was a boy a few years younger than myself; he lived in a place called Moor Bach, a few fields away. He would come on each Saturday and on all school holidays. As he went to a different school to us his holidays were usually a week different to ours and during this week instead of going to school he would come to us and return home at the exact time as if he had been to school, and pretend that he had been.

As summer followed winter there was more and more work to do, and I was by now getting very interested in the jobs that I was given to do by father - these included fetching the cows from the field for milking - twice a day, helping with the milking, of course, cleaning out the cowsheds, stable and pigsty, fetching empty milk churns from the pick-up point by the main road and fetching Maggie, the pony, from the field. First you had to catch her! I would try this in the usual way by tempting her with a morsel in a little bowl but this did not always work as Maggie was getting on a bit and apparently had got wiser with age. Like most horses they would sooner be left in the field than go to work. So when I would approach Maggie with my offering; she would act normally until I got close up, holding out the bait then, with ears back and teeth showing she would go for me - make me run, drop the goodies and she would have whatever it was that was in the bowl 'horse sense' I suppose. If I remember I would then have to get the big stick and chase her into the yard.

I was now around nine years old and was quite a help for my dad, but would like to mention here my mother - she worked hard to bring up us children and at the same time do all the housework, cook the meals and also do a fair amount of work outside; like care for the lesser of the livestock like chickens, ducks, calves etc. So when I did my little bit it helped her as well and I must mention my sisters, Mary, Betty and Audrey; they helped mother I suppose but as I remember, when Betty was old enough to really help - about thirteen - she was sent to or maybe it would be better to say, she was allowed to go to a farm, not too far away called Maes- yr- grove. Mr Morris wanted her to help Mrs Morris with the children, in the mornings and in the evenings after school. It was not so unusual in those days for children of that age to start work, maybe fourteen though. I am not sure whether there would be any real payment for this service - it was her 'keep' which meant her food and her clothing.

There was a story about a man that had lived in Maes-y-grove, prior to Trevor Morris, the man that Betty was to work for. I do not remember or did I ever know his name. I heard a story from my mother (a true story) I think that the events in the story had something to do with where we lived – Broadmoor Farm. The story goes that the man that had farmed Maes-y-grove had brutally murdered his wife, who was apparently found upstairs. It was of course, a very sad and serious incident. Why I remember the story I suppose, is because it had to me as a small boy – a funny side – if one can say that there is a funny side to such a serious event. The funny part came, I suppose, when it was revealed that the murderer was eventually found to be – in those days – 'insane' in Welsh – 'dwl'. However he was sentenced to serve his time or was in fact to be detained at of all places, Broadmoor prison – an appropriate place for a person of that category. When he was informed of his fate, his remarks were, it seemed, "good, I'll be alright there, I'll have plenty of ham and eggs with Jim". Jim, by the way was our predecessor at Broadmoor Farm. The story was, I am sure, true –a sad affair. Our Broadmoor , by the way was not a funny farm!

I was by now becoming quite a little farmer in my own way, as about this time father bought another pony, a two year old, we called her Doll. This meant that father would have to spend more of his time in 'breaking in' Doll. This would take probably a number of weeks as it would involve training on the main road to familiarise it with traffic, as this is where Doll would be used for most of the work. This meant that I had more work to do - farm work is unfortunately a daily job. Most has to be done each day - very little can be left till tomorrow.

Milking the cows had been part of my work for some time - I did this daily before and after school, but now I had another job before school, this was taking the milk to the factory at St Clears in the pony and cart. This trip was shared with our neighbour Jack Morris, Bronhaul, on alternative weeks taking each others milk churns, these were picked up from the milk stands at our farm gate on the main road. So, one week we would take the churns down to the stand, the next week we would collect Jack's churns from the stand on our way to the factory. To me, this meant that I had to collect the full milk churns - ten gallons - off the stand into my cart; not an easy job for a boy of my age - granted all the churns were not full, anyhow, there was as I remember a nasty incident regarding lifting the churns. I would drive the cart to the main road side of the milkstand so that meant that the cart was lower than the stand and I would be lifting the churn down into the cart - easy? Well done! You would think so, but gripping a full milk churn with both hands does not leave any spare limbs to help you if you should trip. Well this is exactly what happened -having got hold of the churn, lifting and moving backwards, I tripped over the tailboard of the cart -the consequences of this should have been - me falling over the edge to the road below and the churn on top of me but I held on to the churn which landed on the cart floor and as it was heavier than me, it saved me from falling - like Kelly's wheelbarrow - eh? Anyway apart from that occasion everything would go all right and I would go on my way, usually in a hurry to be back for school. I can remember other little incidents I suppose, involving some of the regular farmers who were on the same errand as myself. I would pass the school in both directions on my journey; sometimes father would cross the fields and come to meet me - take the pony and cart home and I would go back to school, very often late.

As Ben was eleven years older than me, I cannot remember exactly but he was either working somewhere or he was driving the threshing machine. His job was driving the steam engine or 'traction engine' as these were known. This towed the actual unit from place to place and then supplied the power. During the season the unit would work its way from farm to farm, very often finishing late in the day, and then moving to the next farm - sometimes in the dark. I remember one such occasion, when the thresher was being moved in the dark up to the Moor farm. The road up to the farm was about half a mile across fields and all on a slope, most of which could be seen from our house. My mother, like all mothers I suppose was a great worrier, so you can just imagine all of us watching this slow moving contraption, driven by Ben and guided by helpers, carrying oil lamps. The main problem was a deep drop along the left hand side of the track, one slip, and the whole lot could go tumbling down to the field below. After an agonising spell it reached the safer part of the road and disappeared down into the safety of the farmyard, where it would start another days threshing in the morning.

On the farm the seasons determined the type of work to be done - summer brings the haymaking which is, maybe, the busiest time of all, with very long working days, using all available daylight. Most of the work was done by using horses, as the tractor did not appear till later. Haymaking required many hands, so farmers helped each other during this period, June and July. I was kept home from school for many weeks, it depended on the weather; if it rained, I went to school. So you can imagine, each morning how I wished for a fine day. My job was to lead the cart horses in the hayfield, when moving from one 'tump' to another, also the horse in the 'pitcher' - this operated the grab which picked up the hay off the load and carried it into the hay shed. My father, the pony and me, worked as a unit; the pony pulling the rope that operated the grab, me, leading the pony and father in the hay-shed receiving it and spreading over the shed area. Imagine leading the pony, for maybe eight hours, tiring but sill better than going to school. I would receive one shilling for my days work, but I suppose I valued the food that we had more than that. Our tea meal would be brought out to wherever we were working. There would always be plenty of wholesome food, like fresh bread and butter, nice cheese and as I mentioned earlier 'picks' - these were lovely hot, crisp, crusted currant buns, with melting butter. That was good but supper was the best of all - on the long table in the house - maybe twelve to fourteen men, all tired and hungry but always cheerful as this would be about eleven o'clock.

I cannot remember what effect the absences from school had on my education; I don't think I was that concerned but I remember Mr Jones the headmaster approaching my father suggesting that I be allowed to go to Whitland secondary school.

Our normal school day was quite a long one, walking the three miles to school and again, home. There were no school meals, so we carried our bread and butter and tea in a tin can with a lid - this was called in Welsh a 'sten'. During the dinner hours, we gathered around the classroom fire, maybe seven or eight of us, and we would usually place the tea can on the coal fire to heat it up and very often place a poker across the fire to hold the bread, so that it could be toasted.

I had a fairly regular job to do during the lunch hour. Old aunty Jane Harris, lived not far from the school - we called her aunty but really she was father's aunty. She was at that time about ninety years old. She lived on her own. It was my job, every day, to fetch all the water from the village pump as there was no supply in the house. I carried it in a big can and filled her earthenware containers. I would then take all the ashes from the fire, up the steps to the garden, riddle them, and bring back the 'henlo' - this was the unburnt coal which would be put back on the fire again. This was a daily routine and in addition on Friday, I would go to the post office to collect her old age pension - ten shillings - current value 50p. For this chore I would receive two pence per week which I had to spend on an orange or an apple - I was strictly forbidden to spend it on sweets. As time went by I may have received a little more, but whatever it was I had to place the few coins in the money box provided. The proceeds were intended to contribute towards the cost of some item of clothing. Little did I know then that there was a greater reward, as later on when aunty Jane died I was left the grandfather clock and a chest of drawers. These I have to this day and that was sixty years ago.

I remember one day when old Doctor Jones called at our house; I think it was to do with father, anyhow it must have been necessary as he would have to walk all the way from the road. When he was there mother asked him about me as she was concerned about my 'big breaths'. I suppose one would call it hyperventilating these days. His verdict was that I suffered from a weak heart - just like that - no tests! I suppose in those days one believed the doctor. This fact had a direct effect on my activities for some considerable time. I was, for instance forbidden to play football, to run or take part in any sport. You can just imagine the temptation at school, especially when you were considered to be a reasonable footballer and normally included in the team to play other schools. I did however, on several occasions, take part without any effect on my physical being, but the situation was there for some considerable time. Truthfully now though, I do not believe that there ever was a problem. I am sure that had there been, the many medicals I had later would have discovered it especially during my athletic activities with the RAF. I suppose though thinking back to those day, I must have been a bit of a 'mum's' boy as I have been, reminded of this many times since. The fact that the doctor had said I had a weak heart, probably brought me in favour, although at the time, I was not aware of this. The only other factor that could have accounted for this was that I was the only boy, (Ben I suppose was a man). Both of these factors may have influenced my dad, but I don't think it made much difference to the work that I did; I was never aware of any defect in my health.

As children we made our own play; the girls would play girls games like pretend house (they called it ty bach) or in English little house. I was often left to my own devices when I played. I remember I had at this time, an old bicycle frame and two wheels and although I would have dearly liked to have a bike, the nearest I ever got to this were these three separate items. I did from time to time, find the means of fixing the wheels to the frame but the spindles (made of wood) broke when I put my weight on them. The next modification was to exchange these for metal ones. I was forever trying to master the art of riding it; to accomplish this I would place it alongside the hedge, sit on the seat and push myself along with one foot on the hedge. I practised this for some time and I must have improved as I was going further and further along. Then one day I got as far as the top of the steep slope, where the hedge finished, and as I left the end of the hedge behind me, I gave myself one last long push and I went careering down the slope to crash at the bottom, in the stream.

Not a total success, but it gave me encouragement, as my next objective was to take this contraption on the main road (one big step for mankind), not forgetting that I had neither tyres or tubes, not to mention brakes; so it was with Mary as the only spectator, the demo started with me going down the hill and managing to stay on the seat until Mary shouted from behind me, that there was a car coming - it was a big fib, and as I was in the middle of the road, I swerved to the side, but without tyres the metal wheels slipped sideways and broke the front fork. So that was the end of the 'demo' but worse, that was the end of my bike - back to the drawing board!

Now, back to my work. The summer holidays were much the same then, as now, five weeks. On one of these occasions I was given a five gallon drum of paint and the task of painting every door and window on the farm. I remember I did finish the job; this was more than likely my first contract!

Being born and brought up on a farm, one gets used to animals and I had no fear of any animal, but one day my mind was changed, the fear came from an incident that occurred when I, as I had done before, helped my father castrate the little piglets. I would catch and hold the little pigs, upside down, with their heads between my knees, naturally there would be screams, and the mother sow would be outside the door, very concerned. The 'operation' went all right until father emerged through the door, with the 'product' of the operation in his hand. The mother sow immediately attacked him and he had to run across the yard, chased by the mother sow, with mouth open and making nasty pig noises. Father eventually reached the sanctuary of a low wall and he jumped over to safety. Although I, with some encouragement, or was it a dare from father, chased the sow away, but the effect and indeed the fear, did not leave me for some time.

The other animal that I did have respect for, believe it or not, was a very small dog named Beauty. It belonged to Oswald, my friend, who lived in Bronhaul. I somehow or other got on the wrong side of it, when as boys Oswald and I were playing around pretending to fight. The dog must have thought it was for real and attacked me. After that incident, it would not allow me near Oswald or his house. Later on in life when I owned a dog, I got to know that a boy and his dog can be inseparable.

After the major part of haymaking was over, and the hay was safely 'stacked' in the ricks, there were many associated tasks to be done - for instance - the ricks, had to be made weather/ waterproof for the winter and to this end a lot of lower quality hay had to be cut and gathered from other fields, maybe from where the cows had been grazing. This kind of second rate haymaking, would have to be done by father, with only me to help. I would often be given the job of turning this hay on my own, when father was busy elsewhere. We would gather it in, later in the day, with me making the load on the cart. I have one particular memory of a day when I was turning the hay, using a pitchfork, and being on my own in the middle of this field, on a lovely warm day, I was listening to the grasshoppers making their peculiar noise, so I thought I would silence them by hitting at the spot where I thought they were, in the hay, with a pitchfork. I overdid it a bit and broke one of the prongs of the fork, imagine my dilemma, what was I to tell father who would be using the fork later anyway? I am afraid that I did not report the fact, instead I stuck the fork in the ground, with the broken piece in position, so that father would think that it happened when he removed it. But unfortunately I was asked what I had done with the pitchfork, and why had I not returned it to its place in the toolshed? So, I had to explain what had happened - I felt rather foolish. Also associated with the hay harvest was the final task of thatching the ricks. The material for this was the tall reeds that grew on the riverside. We called it 'hesc', and as we still had our 'share' at the Wityl - remember? It bordered the river. Father would cut this and tie it into sheaves. After one of these occasions, when he had spent most of the day doing this, we went down in the evening, when I came home from school to load up this material and bring it home. This would be after milking, rather late in the day. When we arrived on the scene, it was to find that we were indeed late, as the tide had come up the river, flooded the banks and we saw most of father's days work floating away. Then father had a bright idea - he took the rope from the horses harness, tied it around my waist and I was to wade in to try and retrieve the sheaves. Needless to say, I was terrified, as the brown murky water, with all its floating debris did not appeal to me at all. I seem to remember that we did rescue some of it.

One other memorable occasion was during the same operation but in another year. In this case we did gather all the sheaves and we were halfway home with the load well roped to the cart, with me riding on top. While we were travelling across a slope in the field, I felt the whole load slipping and then realised that we were tipping over - cart - pony - load and of course, me. As father was leading the pony up front, he was the last to know of the problem. However, when he realised what had happened, he came looking for me probably thinking that I was buried under the load. But as the load was roped on I was thrown clear.

My father and mother were capable, each in their own spheres. Father in numerous jobs that had to be done, besides the normal farm jobs. If one considers all the different aspects of work of those days, today for instance, how many people could milk by hand, make a hay rick - round or square, so that it would keep dry during the winter and towards this end thatching was very important. Father was a specialist in this field. His hayricks, when plucked and thatched looked just like a house and were always waterproof and were a point of interest.

I learned a lot from my father and this knowledge was to stand me in good stead later on in life. He was considered, by others, to be an authority in many aspects and they called for his skills. For instance, as well as slaughtering his own pig, he would do the same for most farms around. This was a regular occurrence each year around October/November. It was a time when we, and other farmers, would have free fresh pork. This system worked very well both ways as there would have been far too much fresh pork for one family, so they shared out all the smaller bits of meat that were not to be salted. In this way we all had fresh pork over the two months. You would return the favour when it was your turn. Then there was the other factor, father being the butcher cutting up the pork, he was entitled to a good piece. The day our pig was killed was a sad one, but when you are a farmer you cannot afford to be squeamish. There was a certain amount of preparation like cutting the logs for the fire, that would be made in the corner of the yard, to boil the water that would scald the pig, to remove the hair and scum. The poor old pig had been fed up to fatten it and it had usually become quite docile. When it was led to the slaughter I am fairly sure that it was aware of what was to happen. There was no mention of humane killers in those days. The pig of course provided bacon for the year. As I remember it, it was cut up to provide -two shoulders, two sides and two hams. The hams were usually kept for special occasions, such as haymaking dinners and suppers. It would all be hung from the beams in the kitchen. So with the whole pig to see you through the year, there would be no need to buy any bacon. We had plenty of milk from the cows, eggs from the hen house, but some of the eggs were sold to pay for the hens food. Mother would often bake bread in the big oven, which was fuelled with logs -the vegetables came from the garden, but we had additional potatoes, which were usually grown in one of the big farmers' fields. For this privilege, also the seed potatoes. We had to help clean, weed, and hoe his potatoes during the year and help with the digging and harvesting of the potato crop in the autumn - this was all done by hand.

As we lived a long way from the normal facilities, like doctors etc, mother had to deal with all kinds of emergencies such as minor injuries and she was quite knowledgeable when it came to dealing with these, as I suppose one would learn with experience. I remember one day Mary and I were exploring a rubbish pit and while going down into it, Mary slipped and fell on a broken jam jar. It cut her wrist quite severely on the underside. I suppose these days it would have had several stitches, but mother's treatment was a slice of fat salty bacon applied to it. This did two things, (1) it held the wound together and (2) it stopped the bleeding. I did hear it said also that cobwebs were a good means of stopping bleeding; I did not see any of this used for that purpose, although there was a plentiful supply in the outer buildings. Yet another very memorable act by my mother was when we were playing in our make-believe tent; Mary had an insect in her ear, she naturally ran to mother, who had the presence of mind to put Mary's head on one side and fill here ear with water - lo and behold up floated an ant.

The local doctor from the village would very rarely visit us, in fact we had few visitors. There was 'John the Cwming'; he lived alone in a house not far away, he was apparently an ex naval rating - that would be during the 1914/1918 war -he was rather a mysterious person, very stern and I think we kids were a little wary of him. He was quite friendly with father and mother and he liked a chat and a bit of local gossip. The reasons for his daily visit to our place was to collect drinking water from our pump. He would bring and fill four or five flagons. They were (2 pint beer bottles). We never found out why he could not afford a more appropriate vessel.

Then there was Johnny Morris - he lived in Bronhaul, where we once lived and he worked in the Moor. We were half way in-between his home and his work, but if you remember there was no source of drinking water at Bronhaul, so he would always call, fill his can and sometimes stay for a chat as well. There was Mr Morgan, he was, yes, the man from the Prudential. A certain old man came round selling dried tea -he was called (Twm-Te) in other words, Tom the tea man. He travelled around the countryside calling at all the farms. Then there was a man known as the pack-man. He dealt with clothing -he would carry his pack on his back and unpack it at each location, sometimes for very little return. The other ones that I remember, came only at certain times of the year. They were French men selling onions and we called them 'Shoni Winwns' -in English Shoni the onions. They would come to the door and try to sell the 'hanks', long strings of onions tied together and carried on a yoke on their shoulders. They would only speak in French. Just imagine a Frenchman selling to a Welshman in broken English. Their main phrase was just 'big-moustache" and 'winwns heddi Mari' - a big moustache it appears was their boss who preceded them in days gone by and had given them this password, hoping that he would be remembered. And of course we had the tramps; these varied from the begging type to the ones who were prepared to do little jobs as payment for something to eat and a chance to sleep in the barn. I somehow had a soft spot for tramps, I wished mother would give them something. Mother, I learned later, could have had a different view of tramps as she had apparently had a strange encounter. She told a true story of the time when she first got married and lived with father in the Bont. It appears that the main road, close by, was well known for tramps as it was somehow a route from one depot to another. The story as mother told it goes something like this.

One morning as she was still in bed, about seven o'clock, after father had gone to work, the bedroom door slowly opened, and a man peeped around the door. Mother apparently, although very frightened, challenged him, and asked him who he was. He said that he wanted something to eat, and asked what the time was. Mother insisted that he leave immediately and he went slowly out of the room, down the stairs and put on his boots which he'd taken off before going up. Then mother asked him how he had got into the house, he said that the door was open. This was not strictly true - the door had a latch similar to the old stable door latch, but mother said that the thumb part of the latch was missing and had been replaced by a wooden one. So when father had gone to work, he had removed this 'key' hidden it close by and it was thought that the tramp had seen father hide the latch and had used it. Fortunately soon after the tramp left the insurance man arrived and mother, you can imagine, was glad of the opportunity to tell someone of her experience. He in turn reported the incident and it appears the tramp was found and he had on him, some items of clothing which he had stolen from another lady's clothes line.

Mother would often tell us of her younger days and of her mother and father as they had died before I was born. Mother had very little spare time but at the end of the day, we would sit around the fire usually a log fire, she had in those day, long dark auburn hair, and she liked the girls Betty or Mary to comb her hair and she would at the same time relate some of her stories. I well remember another true tale involving my grandmother, who lived in Bronhaul, in Llanddower (mother's old home). In those days people would take wool to the weaving mill, to make material which would then be made into clothing. My grandmother was to make such a journey, which involved walking, carrying the wool - from her home to Bronwydd, a distance of approximately sixteen miles each way. To be able to accomplish such a journey it was necessary to start at dawn. So it would be appropriate to go to bed very early the previous night. This she did. Remembering in those days that clocks were only for people who could afford them and they could not; so it was more or less early, late, etc. Grandmother, it seems, went to bed during daylight, and went to sleep, fully intending to get up before it became daylight next day. Unfortunately when she woke up, it was fully daylight; she was most concerned and lost very little time in preparation, like breakfast. She was soon on the road and I suppose, trying to make up for lost time, if that was possible, with a load of wool to carry. The story goes, however, that when she had reached halfway she realised that it was getting darker, and it was only then that she realised that she had not slept late, but had woken up not long after going to sleep on the same day. As it was now getting nearer night, she managed to find a place to sleep in a place called Sarnau Farm on the roadside. Apparently she slept in the barn and carried on her journey in the morning. Such events seem to be in this day and age, unbelievable, but it was a hard time and a hard life and a true story.

Broad Moor was a long way from Llanddowror, where mother and father originated from, but in spite of this father remained true to his faith, and Elim Chapel, where he had been as a young man. He would on occasions cycle the five or six miles each way, usually on communion Sundays once a month. He was by now a Deacon and he remained so until the end of his days.

As children we were brought up to respect religion, and although we were not aware of it at the time, I know that it has had an effect on my life and it has brought a lot of comfort in different ways. We went to Sunday school quite often to the Congregational Chapel in St Clears; in fact it was next door to our day school and was called Capel Mair, where I was later made a member. We sometimes went to chapel in the evenings and this was something that we liked to do as there was very little in the way of 'life' in Wales on a Sunday anyway.

At home the wireless had not been thought of, not by us anyway - that came much later. I well remember when it was introduced; it came by way of our cousin Ivor from Cardiff He was, remember the one that fell out with Ben over the hay, at Bronhaul. He continued to visit us during the summer holidays and it was during one of these visits that he brought the wireless. I remember him carrying it on his shoulders, because, if you remember, our house could not be approached by car - even if you had one! We would have this wireless for the duration of the holidays. Incidentally, that was not all Ivor brought with him; he was now a grown up and has some regular girlfriends. So life did get a little more exciting during this period. Back to the wireless and the reason for mentioning it.. On Sunday there was a Welsh sermon and this was my father's favourite programme; during this service we as children, had to sit quietly throughout the service. Can you imagine the situation - difficult - sometimes one of us would find it hard not to laugh about something and this would have an effect on all of us, also Ben was not beyond starting such an incident. It would, however, be brought under control by my father who was listening intently to the sermon. That was our first introduction to the wireless. It was many years later that we owned a radio. This was with a wet accumulator and a dry battery and a smaller dry battery.

It must be remembered that during the whole period of my childhood we did not once have electric power. All lighting was from paraffin lamps, with hurricane lamps for outside. Oh yes, going upstairs to bed meant lighting a candle. This was apparently one aspect of our life that Ivor and his girlfriend found 'different' also our toilet, when we had one, would be outside. The famous remark when one wanted to 'go' - I have to go for a country one!

Ben was by now, somewhere around nineteen to twenty years old, and like Ivor I suppose had also met a young lady - her name was Dilys, and he was later to marry her. Ben, if you remember, drove the threshing machine, the one that was taken around the various farms, and it was at one of these locations that he discovered Dilys, in Merrivale Farm. He must have had the ordinary period of courtship but I do not remember much about it as I don't suppose he would discuss it with his ten year old brother. One thing I do remember, is when he first brought Dilys home, we children had to be in bed before they arrived.

I was about ten years old at this time, and at this time Ben must have finished the threshing season. Father had purchased a motorbike to travel to and from his work, and as I remember, father was unwell and Ben had jumped at the chance of driving the steam roller, as he was already a steam engine driver. After a while, father recovered and he decided to pay Ben a visit, using the motorbike. He was returning from this visit at a road junction, near Abergwili. On entering the main road, he was in collision with another vehicle. He suffered injuries to his head and face and was in hospital for some considerable time. This unfortunately left its mark on his face the rest of his life.

Once more, mother and I were without father or Ben. Poor Mother - this was father's third accident and Ben had also had his accident remember? Fathers first accident was when he had his ribs broken when he fell on a fifty six pound weight, during his pig slaughtering days. His second was when he suffered a broken jaw as a result of the handle on a heavy hay press, slipped and caught him under the chin - and now another one! This then meant that Ben had to remain on the roller, which he did for a long time. In fact for the rest of his working life. Father when he recovered, spent his time at home, The fact that father was at home, for what seemed to be a permanent period, I remember that he would take the milk to the factory more often, and my school attendance time looked a bit better.

I remember a few incidents regarding fathers journey to St Clears with the milk. He would use Doll the young pony, which he had recently 'broken' as opposed to Maggie, the pony that I used. Now, father I believe, was rather absent-minded or you could say, often preoccupied. So I can imagine him sitting in the trap, thinking maybe, of some problem, and not necessarily paying much attention to the driving of the pony. Whether the pony realised this or not, is doubtful, but it decided to take the bit between its teeth and bolt, Although not much harm was done, the pony seemed to make a habit of this and it occurred several times in the future.

I would of course do my usual trip to the factory on Saturdays and Sundays, I remember a very funny incident that occurred on my return journey one Saturday morning - funny maybe - but it could have been serious. Leslie, who I mentioned earlier, was the boy who came to play. He came every Saturday, without fail. He was a little younger than me, but his ambition in life seemed to be to do all the things that I did. On this particular Saturday, he had accompanied me on my trip to the factory. We were returning and nearing home, and as we had left the main road, I would allow him to take control of the driving. Here I must explain a few points. First the trap that we had was a spring trap - therefore while travelling over rough, rutted tracks, one was thrown around a bit. This was normal and was accepted but Leslie was not satisfied with standing in the trap, he stood on a runner, immediately behind the pony and as we were crossing the stream, over the bumpy stones, all of a sudden Leslie disappeared down between the pony and the trap, into the stream below. Although he was soaking wet, he was not really hurt - except his pride.

Leslie was in some ways different from us, I suppose it must have been his upbringing. He did not have a father, as such, but a grandad who lived with his mother. His outlook on life was rather different to ours in so far as he would, for instance, stay away from school, especially on days when we were at home. He did, if you remember, go to a different school; his absence did not go unnoticed - it attracted the attention of the attendance officer. We had from time to time tried to frighten Leslie, by saying that if he did not go to school the officer would come and take him to an approved school. So, you can imagine the situation when, indeed, the attendance officer did come and catch him one morning, not far from our house. You could hear Leslie shouting, 'Mam, Mam' (that would be for mother of course) when he was being taken away, not to an approved school but to his normal day school. This did improve his attendance for a while. School, for me at this time, was more interesting, as I was involved in games with the older boys and I was also interested in some of the older girls, as one is at this age, all very innocent though. The games played by the boys in those days, all came in season. Football, cricket, conkers, tops and whips and marbles. Your prestige went up and down according to how many you had conkered (conquered) this was played with chestnuts - not the girls! The one thing that always seemed to be in season was hoops - these ranged from tyres to iron rings, with a driving hook. You drove them to school, you raced with them at school and you drove them home when you had finished. This reminds me of another incident which happened to me. My friend Oswyn, who lived in the village, had brought his big tyre and he would usually keep it at the back of a house near the school but on this particular day, he brought it into the playground, and when he had finished with it, he asked me to take it to its parking place. To accomplish this I had to go out onto the main road and as I did not own a hoop; I was not really qualified, nor capable of controlling such a 'vehicle' at such speeds. It was in other words - out of control. Unfortunately at that very same time a farmer was passing, driving a heavy horse, my tyre went straight for the horses front legs and brought it down, It was a disaster but there was not much one could do really, the horse was soon up and - ready to go, I recovered the tyre and went back to school, but my friend did not trust me with his tyre again. Needless to say the farmer was not pleased!

Saint Clears was a fairly big village and I suppose I was growing up in it or should I say, just outside it. It had all the necessities of life I suppose and apart from the annual sports day and the Michelmas Fair there was not much more to it, for children anyway. I had never seen a town, as such and it was to be several more years before I would go to see a film, so for the time I suppose, we enjoyed what we had.

My life's ambition, at this time, was to own a proper bike and a watch. That I felt, would make me the happiest boy in the world, but of course I had yet to earn these. I suppose if you live a simple life, you will only aim for simple things. I just remembered another experience I had at the local fair in St Clears, This was one of the few occasions when we had a few pennies to spend. I must have been attracted to a water pistol, which I saw on sale on one of the stalls, So, can you imagine, remember, I had never owned one before, heres me going around a crowded fair, looking for someone that I knew, to have a 'go' at, It was most unfortunate for me, that this person, should be a fairly near neighbour of ours, who liked his pint, and at the time that I encountered him, he had already had a few - well how was I to know this! He looked straight at me, and I thought 'what a chance' and I discharged my loaded pistol, straight into his face. Apart from being temporarily blinded, he was infuriated and I can safely say, that I had to spend the rest of my time in the fair avoiding Mr James as he was bent on catching me.

During my childhood, I can hardly remember an incident when I was really in trouble regarding my behaviour, but I can remember one evening when my sisters, Mary, Betty, Audrey and I, had, as we sometimes did, been playing in the moonlight; it involved chasing each other around the hay-ricks. I still cannot remember what we did wrong, however, when we went in later, Father took each of us out separately, and to all intents have a good telling off - all except me and I never found out why. Although I never believed it at the time, it was considered that I was a bit of a favourite. Now looking back, maybe I was. I know I was great friends with my mother, and from a fairly young age, I dreaded the day when she would die. I could be very moody at times and my mother could always tell, as she said that I always pulled the peak of my cap down over my eyes. When I was in a mood, or had been crossed, I liked to go somewhere on my own. I remember, I had my mother worried one day, when I escaped to a favourite place of mine; the field next to the house which had long grass, as it was kept for hay. I would go and lie in the middle of this. I still think that there is a no more tranquil place, than in the middle of a growing hay-field. However, on this occasion it worried mother, as she did not know where I was, until I appeared later. Because Ben and I were so many years apart in age I remember him more as a grown up and that he played the harmonica; my mother believe it or not had taught him to play. He had by now, been courting Dilys for some time and needless to say, he spent more of his evenings out. I do not remember exactly when, but about this time, Ben actually bought a new motorbike.

Unfortunately, when it was delivered, mother or father had no idea that he had bought it (the cost in those days was around £28) so they instantly gave instructions to return it, so Ben did not even see it. Soon after this Ben and Dilys were to get married, an important occasion you would think; well in those days it was something that had to be done and as it was not a church service, there was very little fuss and I was not involved. Ben was still roller driving and as I mentioned earlier a van was provided for accommodation purposes. For some time Dilys did live with Ben in the van, then the time came when she became pregnant and she lived with us at Broad Moor and Ben would return at weekends.

When the baby was born, it was a boy and they named him Gwilym. There is good reason for me to remember his birth, as I was the one who went for the doctor across the fields to Saint Clears. I was by now eleven years old and as Ben was eleven years older than I, I was now eleven years older than Gwilym. Dilys and Gwilym were to spend the next few years with us. When Gwyilym was a little bit older, he would always wait for my father returning from the milk run from Saint Clears, as he would usually have a packet of sweets. Later on in life Ben and Dilys were to make their home in Abergwili. This is where Gwilym started school.

So with Ben gone from home and Betty in Maesygrove so, Mary, Audrey and myself, were the nearest in age, and we probably spent more time together as children. Mary, by the way being only sixteen months younger than myself I had by now got familiar with the job I had been doing for years - like cleaning cowsheds, digging the garden, sweeping the yard and cutting sticks - yes I was now trusted with the chopper! Father would usually allocate me a job, like digging the garden and he would tell me how much I had to do, and I would be expected to finish the job - I usually did. On Saturdays, when returning from the milk factory, I would call at a place which made 'pele' for the fire. This was black material, made from coal dust, which was mixed with clay and water, very much like cement. This would be used for the fire, it was slow burning and lasted a long time. Sometimes we made the pele at home. I usually ended up doing it on Saturday afternoons. The coal dust was the remains of a load of coal, which we had delivered occasionally and the clay was the 'cement' I suppose. This clay was obtained originally from an appropriate part (wet part) of land. It was raised as they do Peat, in spadefuls - it was then left to dry around the eaves of the barn, then it could be beaten with a mallet to break it up into fine powder. This was then mixed with the coal dust - water was added and after some more thorough mixing, it would then be ready for the fire. I used to mix sufficient for the week. As an alternative to using clay, you could use cement, but you can imagine the difference, it would of course set hard, so you had to form it into little balls before it set.

I was now nearly twelve years old, becoming quite capable of doing most of the work around the farm and I was very aware and indeed, proud of the fact that I was able to do it. I was also aware that I was getting older and as such, expected to do them whereas at eight or nine years old, it was a far greater achievement, as it was unusual. Sunday was a day of rest and apart from the 'must do's' all other work was left till Monday.

As children, we were apparently all born at home and the midwife would attend at each birth, and from what I have been told, mother did not at any time, go away from home for the births. The midwife I mentioned was Mrs James {Sofia) she was from a small farm called The Mountain, in Welsh it was pronounced 'Mwntan' -it was a few miles away. The fact that she had attended mother so many times they had become more or less friends. So the visits now, were more or less social ones.

One other lady that visited us occasionally was Miss Bowen 'Cwymbryn'. Her visit would be infrequent as I think she was restricted in her 'wanderings' by her family. The reason for this acquaintanceship was that she lived close to Penrallt - remember - where I was born. She was unfortunately a little simple, this was well known by all her friends. When she came to us she would always say that she was staying overnight and mother had to do a lot of persuading to get her to go home. One thing that used to work though was that she liked my brother Ben, he was of course a lot younger than her, but she would go if Ben went part of the way with her - this was of course before Ben got married. She was as I remember, quite harmless and as we had been brought up to respect such people, we got on well with her.

All the places that we had lived in up to now, were rented and leased. We had now been living in Broad Moor for seven years. It was owned by a Mr and Mrs Husband, they had farmed it prior to us taking over, but they had now moved to Swansea. They as landlords, decided about this time that they wanted to sell the farm, so once more father was on the look out for another similar farm. After some time he found a place called Cwrt-y-Bedw in Llangynog about ten or twelve miles away. For the next year, we were to have two places at the same time. One consideration that most people would not realise, is that farming requires the proceeds of one season to support the next. For instance, the summer provides the hay that is harvested for the winter. So with two places this applied in both cases. In the summer time we had two haymaking seasons! So I found myself travelling back and for with father, to work all day at Cwrt-y-Bedw and return most times in the dark. Father decided that he would have a sale, to get rid of the stock and other articles at Broad Moor, and then he would re-stock Cwrt-y-bedw.

It was rather a sad thought, to think that after seven years, we were to leave Broad Moor, leaving friends that you had lived with, like Johnny Morris. John Cumming, and his bottles - remember? Of course the whole family would be affected - school etc. I remember John Cumming made a little rhyme about our move and it went like this:-

When this barly sale is over
Oh, how happy I shall be,
When I get to Cwrt-y-Bedw,
No more selling milk for me.

Not strictly true, but appropriate at the time. The extra work involved at Cwrt-y-Bedw gave father a reason to involve me more and more. I was by now over twelve possibly approaching thirteen, not yet though - and I felt I had been working for many years. I had I suppose, so much so, that I did not think it unreasonable when father took me to Cwrt-y-Bedw to a field of mown hay. He took me there in the morning and left me there to turn a whole field of hay on my own. I well remember that it was a very warm day (hay making weather); I started turning the first turn around by the hedge, and I was to go round and round all day, till I would end up in the middle, which I did about five or six o'clock. In the meantime I remember I had a stop for sandwiches around midday, oh yes, I remember a neighbour called with a drink. I suppose he felt sorry for me. He told my father later that he would never have believed, that I could have turned a whole field of hay on my own, but of course father knew better - didn't he?

Looking back at this phase in my life, I believe more and more in the old saying 'you are as old as you feel' - I was then working as hard as I could, to be at a level that I thought, that all boys of my age should be at, but of course I now realise that not all boys were as 'advanced'. This thought alone, made me try harder - it is I suppose up to your parents to make you aware of these facts. From reading this story, one may get the impression that father was a hard man, of course I would say he was not. My association with him was based solely on respect. I never ever felt that I was forced to do anything, on the contrary I felt that it was a privilege and I was proud that he had trusted me.

My relationship with my mother was entirely different. This was based on motherly affection I suppose. I was very close to her and mother was always concerned that father did not consider my age, especially when I was around eight or nine years old. Mother, if you remember, was a dressmaker, and had earned her living, doing just this before she was married. Afterwards, although she still had her sewing machine, she did not have the time to do much sewing. As a housewife, mother, farmers wife, etc, she had very little time for anything else. One title I missed out; she was also an 'agony aunt' to several of the local wives and spinsters; they all appreciated her advice and confidentiality.

At the end of that summer, we were to leave Broad Moor, and move to Cwrt-y-Bedw; that was, mother, father, Mary, Audrey and myself Although it was always exciting to move to a new place, this time it was a little different as we had the memories of what was probably the most impressive period of our young lives, as so much had happened during those years at Broad Moor. Cwrt-y-Bedw was very different; it was, you could say, off the beaten track; it was literally on unsurfaced roads, as many country roads were in those days – red stone – was quite pleasant really. The traffic was only farm vehicles with the exceptional car. There was no bus service during the week but the bus came past on Saturdays morning to take people to Carmarthen and return at lunch time. We had then, not only left Broad Moor but we had left our village with its school, shop etc. This meant that Mary and Audrey were to start a new school 'Llangynog'. This was in a very small village. I was nearly at school leaving age, so I was to attend the same school in St Clears which was now some six or seven miles away. To me at first this was exciting as I had to cycle each day too and fro', especially as I had just started riding a bike – remember?

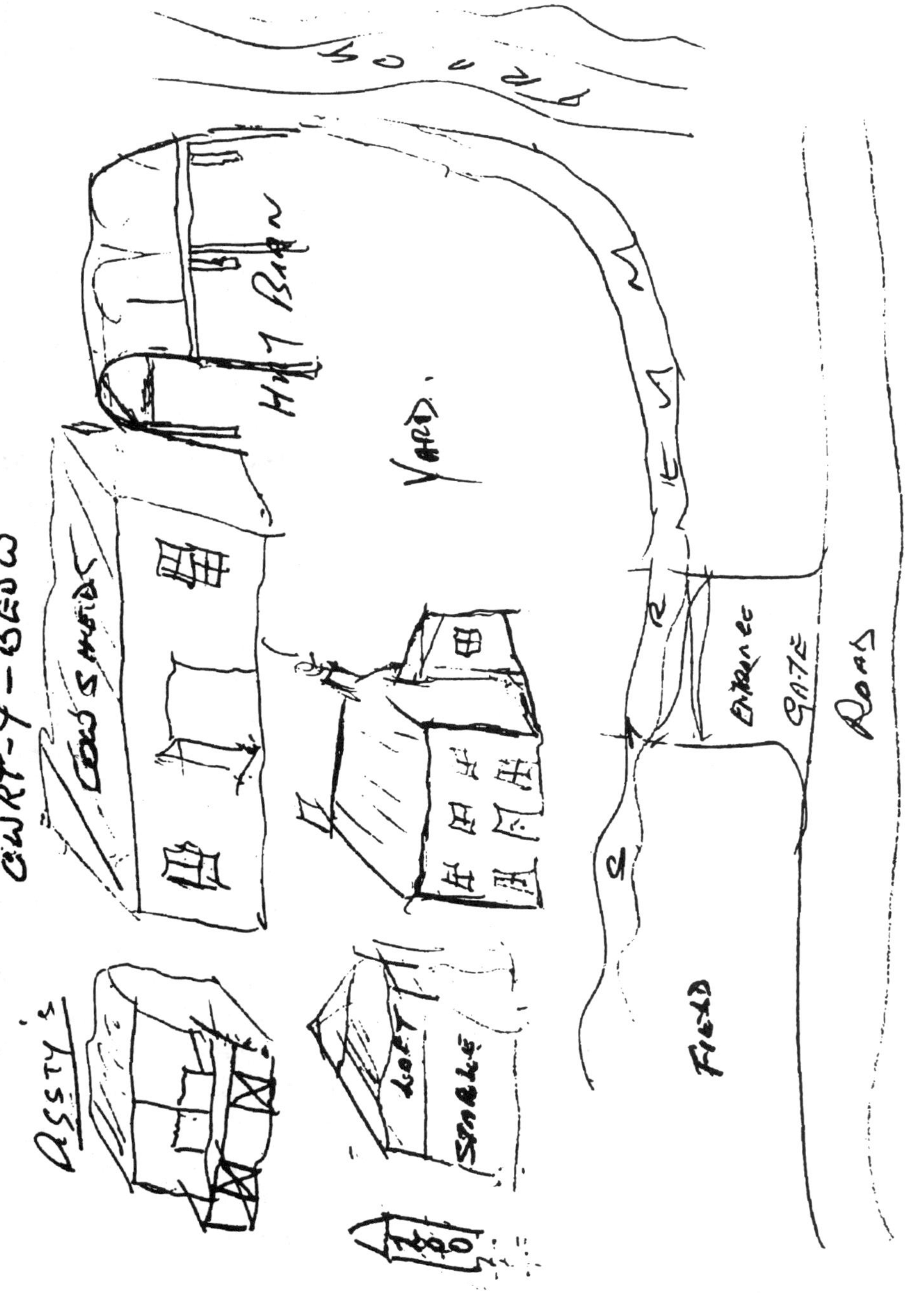

CWRT-Y-BEDW
COW SHEDS
HAY BARN
YARD
ENTRANCE
GATE
ROAD
FIELD
LOFT
STABLE

Slowly we all settled into our new environment, each in his own way. This of course applied to father and mother as well, as all neighbours were new and strange. Cwrt-y-Bedw was a fairly recently built place. It was built of stone and brick, that was one of the things that I liked about the place. Things continued like this for a while. Father had now re-stocked with cows but as I remember it, he did sometimes go away to work, on a kind of casual basis. A little later he had a contract with the County Council, carting road stone from a quarry, to stock piles along the road. I remember he bought another bigger horse for this job. Life had changed for me; no more taking milk to the factory before school, it took me all my time to get there for nine in the mornings. Oh yes, I just remembered a lorry came each day to collect it from outside our gate - I was sorry really.

I was now alas, nearly fourteen years old and about to leave school. If you remember I was reluctant to grow up, but there was nothing I could do about it, because when I eventually left school, I was no longer a little boy and not yet a man, rather a confusing time. And yet I remember I soon came to like Cwrt-y-Bedw, and it became quite a milestone in my young life. Looking back at that time, I think the reason for this was that in this old world, you have to belong somewhere and as long as I was at school, I felt that I belonged there but when I left I had to belong somewhere else and Cwrt-y-Bedw was that somewhere else. Don't forget at this stage of life you are not in control of your destiny, this makes it more confusing. Being at home, not going to school each day, I became more interested in the work that I was involved in, I think that I was seeing things that needed doing, as opposed to doing the things that you were told to do.

Our predecessor at Cwrt-y-Bedw, had left a lot of things undone and consequently, we had to do a lot of things to catch up. Farm work is strictly seasonal, for instance in the winter, you had to get rid of the heap of cow muck that had accumulated as a result of cleaning out the animal sheds. This was taken to the fields. You do this in the winter when the ground is hard with frost, this allowed the horse cart to travel over the ground without making deep ruts. Cart wheels in those days were, narrow wooden ones with iron bands (not rubber tyres as we have today) the muck was spread over the fields to make the grass grow - usually hay fields. The muck heap included very often, the sweepings from the stone farmyard; this contained various foreign objects which would damage hay cutting machines, so in the spring, that was another seasonal job, picking stones etc, from the fields that were intended for hay.

Springtime on the farm, is a most wonderful time and this one was also 'the springtime of my life'. Everything is growing after the long winter, the cows can now go out to graze, as the grass is plentiful, and the other, yes - exciting event - is that the cows can be left out at night. When neighbouring farmers were working in the fields, you could hear the clonking of the steel horse drawn rollers, as they rolled the field on a lovely warm summers day - it was a lovely feeling.

CHAPTER III

FARMING YFARS

Life seemed to be changing for me now. I was I suppose, rather small for my age but as I had finished school, I got my very first pair of long trousers, and that alone in those days was a sign of growing up. This is now an experience denied youngsters these days, as even toddlers are dressed in long trousers to imitate grown-ups.

Our new neighbours were naturally all small farmers. There was Manllwyd, Crose-y-ceilog, Croes-y-celiog Fawr and Castell. In Manllwyd, there was Douglas, a boy of my own age. In Croes-y- ceilog, there was Sally, a girl of my age, who I liked very much, and the Castell was to have a very different attraction as I was to end up working there for Gomer Thomas. I apparently had to start earning my living, father and Gomer came to an arrangement for me to go and work there on a temporary basis, until I got a more permanent job. I would receive payment for this, but payment in those days included board and lodge - that meant that you lived in and had your food there. In actual money, I would receive about five shillings a week, this in today's currency would be twenty five pence, yes twenty five pence a week. Looking back at the fairly brief period that I worked there, I think it was not a favourable experience for a young boy starting work. The family consisted of, Mrs Thomas, the daughter, and Gomer, the son. There were other daughters, but they had left home. The work that I had to do was not difficult, as I had been taught from a very early age and I was glad that I had. I did not really like it there but it would not be right to say so. I think that I liked Mrs Thomas least of all as I thought (even with no experience of such situations) that she was mean and not very friendly. I remember that at meal times she would have jam and cheese on the table, and she could say that you could choose, but you could not have both. There was one rather unpleasant incident that I did not forget and this is it: I had been working in the field, trashing the hedge and I had spotted a kind of walking stick growing in the hedge, I cut it out and trimmed it and I was quite pleased with it. I had it then around the place for a few days, and when I went down to my home, Cwrt-y-Bedw, one night, I left if there for my father I suppose. Old Mrs Thomas asked me the next day what had happened to it, as I did not think that it mattered all that much, I did not tell her that I had left it at home. I thought that if she really wanted it I would bring it back that evening, but Mrs Thomas was not satisfied, she gave me time off work to go and look for it. So without informing her I went down home, picked up the walking stick, took it back and there waiting for me was Mrs Thomas! Of course, she knew all along that I had taken it home (big deal). Another strange experience for me was regarding the daughter; she was about thirty five years old. I had heard from my mother, that she was having an affair. No one knew for certain whether this was true. During my early days there I told my mother that I thought that she was pregnant - how did I know, you may ask? Well from her behaviour I suppose. She probably thought that I was too young to notice her, well I was not. The strangest thing of all was that when the day came for it all to happen, her mother had not realised that she was pregnant. She turned her out of the house and she had to be helped across the field to Maenllwyd, where her sister lived - that does not say much for the old lady, does it? I was probably right about her in the first place.

In my young days, tramps were fairly common and they could be classed as - local - or strangers. During my time in the Castell, I was to encounter two local tramps. One was John Barleycorn and the other Jack Protheroe. I say encounter, as my first experience of jack Protheroe was, early one morning, when I went into a place where hay was stored, and as I was actually fetching hay for the calves, I plunged the pitchfork into the heap and had the fright of my life, when out jumped John. I later gathered that this was not an unusual occurrence. I was to see him many times after that but I never knew when. It appears that he would seek work on the farms, earn the money, and disappear to drink it all, returning when he ran out. John Barleycorn was very much the same; he would work on the farm and he was probably longer at work and spent less time away than John Protheroe. He was a very good hard worker.

Gomer, the son was really the person that I was involved with work-wise, but I did not think that he was much good as a boss. Maybe I had got used to my father's ways - the difference in attitude could, I suppose be that father had worked for bosses in his earlier years and had learned from that, while Gomer had never worked for anyone except maybe, his father - that's a thought! Gomer hardly ever explained anything, not even the jobs he wanted me to do. A typical instance that must have made an impression on me was - he would pick up some tools and tell me to bring the rest and he would remark 'come with me', and we would end up in some field, and I would have no idea of the job until we got there.

As a boy, I was to all intents and purposes, doing a man's job and with hindsight it now seems, managing it fairly well but it must be realised that at times, however well I managed, there were occasions and certain kinds of work, that demanded a man's strength – a quality that in spite of all my ability, I did not have at the age of fifteen. This fact was brought very much to mind and I have never forgotten this specific job where it became evident.

Working for Gomer in the Castell was my very first experience of employment. I have already related my experiences while I was there so bearing this in mind, one can probably understand my predicament. I would describe Gomer as an unqualified employer. This specific job that I refer to was to do with harvesting – all of which was done in those days of the 'thirties' with horses. Horse drawn machines were used to harvest the various crops, hay corn, etc. In ideal circumstances and on larger farms, a machine we referred to as a Reaper and Binder was used but the smaller or medium sized farmer did not have this luxury.

The binder as it was normally referred to was drawn by three horses, side by side as a team. The binder not only cut the corn, it also, by means of the process within, gathered the crop and deposited it in measured bundles referred to as sheaves – these were each wrapped with twine and tied securely – hence the name binder. Later on in my farming years, I became more familiar with the binder on the big farms. I remember, even then, being intrigued with the fact that a mechanical contraption could be made to tie a knot.

On smaller farms a binder would not be available, as there would not be sufficient work for it. Secondly it would be to expensive. Such equipment as mowing machines that were normally used to mow hay could be and were used to a limited degree to cut the small amount of corn that was sometimes grown on smaller farms. When used for cutting corn, the mowing machine was adapted by the use of additional equipment fixed to the knife bar to imitate the function of a binder. The result was basically the same, except that the sheaves had to be tied by hand later. The equipment for adapting the mower from hay cutting to corn cutting consisted of a slatted platform, fitted directly behind the knife bar, parallel to the ground. It was hinged and operated by foot pedal. The platform was raised to an angle and prevented the corn from dropping off until the pedal was released to the flat position again, leaving the corn in untied sheaves.

This equipment required an extra man to operate the pedal and use an off-set rake to manage the corn – this would be in addition to the normal driver whose job was to drive the horses and keep the machine on course.

You may now be wondering where I was involved in all this and where I thought I was lacking in strength and ability. I was responsible, while sitting alongside the other man, for driving the horses and keeping the machine on course. I was at that age, fifteen, small I suppose, although I was strong but not strong enough for the job that I was now involved in. Namely, controlling two large horses, a job I had done before. The difference was that these horses were walking alonside, what was to them tempting food and as it seemed, pinching mouthfuls of corn. It turned out to be an 'eat as you go' situation. The effort of reaching for the mouthfuls affected the line of travel and this in turn affected the proper width that the machine was cutting but most of all it affected Gomer, my boss alongside me, who had from the outset impressed on me not to allow this to happen! The question was – how do you stop a hungry horse grabbing mouhtfuls of its favourite food whilst in among'st it? This situation continued in spite of my best efforts to prevent it and in spite of the continual instruction I was getting from a very frustrated Gomer, who was using his hands and his feet and if I may say, at times, language that I was not familiar with. Although the situation improved as the day progressed this could have been due to several factors. (1) did Gomer give up instructing me? (2) did the horses have their filll of corn or indeed, as I would like to think, I improved in my effort. This was an experience that I have never forgotten

Sometimes my work took me a long way from the farm itself, but yet in sight of it, so when I was sent to work there I would have no idea of the time but we had an arrangement that at the required time Gorner would place a brightly coloured garment or rag, on a pole, as a signal for me to return - a kind of silent semaphore I suppose.

I was pleased, in a way I suppose, that my job here was not a permanent one. Not too long after this, I was to finish my time. I am not sure how long I had been there - a rough guess - six months. It came to an end, I think, because they could do without me. So, for a short period I was to be at home again.

Now, I think, the best way to explain the next phase in my life would be to refer back to the other place where we lived - Broad Moor, because when I was there I remember I spent a lot time helping with the haymaking etc. in The Moor, a bigger farm that joined ours. About the time that we left Broad Moor, Polly, the daughter of Mrs Davies, The Moor, got married to a Mr Bowen - nothing strange in this except that they were probably in their forties. Before this Polly was really the 'Farmeress'. Her mother Mrs Davies, was past her farming days, so that the men folk required to run the farm were hired from year to year. The year started and finished at Michaelmas. Michaelmas Fair fell on the 12th October in St Clears and the Carmarthen Fair, which was the county town, was on the 14th November. Both these fairs were hiring fairs. So the period of employment went from one Michaelmas to the next. There were few variations to this arrangement - for instance, you would not move every year. Very often the same person would work in the same farm for many years. This was of course by mutual agreement of salary and conditions. In the Moor, they would have two farm servants, as they were called. Coming back to my situation at this time, little did I know that I was destined to be one of the servants at the Moor, but not yet, as I was too small and too young to replace a fully developed manservant.

In spite of this I kept in contact by spending periods of time, helping out in busy periods. I really liked working there and I was really disappointed when these periods came to an end, when I would go off home again for a while.

I remember on one occasion, Mr Bowen came to my home Cwrt-y-Bedw, to see father and mother, to arrange for another spell of work for me at the Moor. It was arranged that I would have seven shillings a week; when Mr Bowen asked me if that was sufficient, my mother said 'that I would gladly work there for no pay at all' - true, I suppose. I remember on another occasion, when I left the Moor to go home, Mr Bowen said, 'You can come back at Christmas'. This was just to please me I suppose, but I was that naive that when Christmas came, I was on my way there again! I was by now fifteen years old and it was time that I got some permanent employment. I could not work in the Moor - I was too young, so Mr Bowen had a good idea. Although I did not know it at the time, his sister had a farm called Frongelly, on the other side of Carmarthen, on the Bronwydd road. It was a newly built farmhouse and buildings and Mrs Jones, his sister, lived there with her two daughters, Phillys and Nesta. Phillys was seventeen years old and Nesta was still at school. Mr Jones apparently, had been killed in an accident a few years previously. Mrs Jones required a farm labourer to cope with the farm work and it appears that Mr Bowen thought that I could fill this situation. It was agreed that I should go there on an agreed annual salary of fifteen pounds. I should explain here that the reason that I was suitable for Mrs Jones and too young for Mr Bowen was that Frongelly was a smaller farm - approximately sixty acres - and did not have some of the heavy jobs that you have on big farms - ploughing for instance, this was to come. Nevertheless, I was the only 'man' on the place.

It was now nineteen thirty three, I was just over fifteen years old, and just starting out on my first real job. I now felt grown up - the test was yet to come! Mrs Jones was a member of a large family and she had several brothers and sisters around the area, near Abergwilli. My first impression of her was very favourable, and I soon became settled in. She treated me like the family, there was always plenty of good food; this was an important factor, especially when it is considered that it is part of your payment and it was to be for a year. The other factor to be considered was that a lad of fifteen gets mighty hungry. To explain the system of hiring I have already mentioned the food, the other was your accommodation. You slept either 'in' or 'out' - this meant, in the house or out, usually in a loft, over the cows or the stable. It was thought that the warmth from the animals kept the loft warmer, this sounds a bit ancient, but true I suppose. My bedroom at Frongelly was over the stable, as the whole farm was recently built, all the buildings were new. My room was constructed in one of the corners of the loft from all nice clean matchboards. Inside there was a bed, a chair and shelves to hold whatever, and of course 'your box'. This was important - it was a type of metal trunk and it was a kind of symbol - it contained all your possessions, as it was the first thing collected when you came and the last thing taken away by your employer when you left. It meant - you had come or you had gone! So, it was always important to consider all things relating to your board and lodge, as you would say today. There was one great advantage in sleeping out and that was privacy. My room was cleaned and bed made regularly, usually by Phillys the daughter. It was comfortable enough.

When one thinks of board and lodge, I now realise that the cost could be far more than the money you receive. One last word about salary - it was per year and during the year you asked for 'bits' as you required it.

When you start work at a new place, it takes a while to get into the routine of work. This is usually not difficult it you take a lead from someone who is already there, but here of course there was no one. So you pick up the routine day by day and week by week and as it is usually repetitive, you should soon become used to it. Farm work is a daily pattern which involves the daily routine like - milking, morning and evening, feeding the animals, cleaning and bedding them down. In between is when other jobs are done, mostly out in the fields, this in turn goes with the seasons.

Starting in a new place, like I did here, I could liken the situation to two boxers in a ring, for the first time sizing each other up (that is a bit extreme really), but the idea is the same. I more or less accepted Mrs Jones and the situation, but I discovered that the trust was not the same from her. This only became evident after I had been there for a few weeks. One day I found a complete box of matches, just outside the barn door - neatly placed - or so it seemed. No one on the premises smoked and there was no obvious use for these, so I came to the conclusion that this had been placed there to test my honesty. I do not suppose that I realised it at the time but later I did. Being me, I just picked them up and returned them to Mrs Jones; 'How did they get there?' was the only remark - I wonder!

Frongelly was a modern farm, especially the farm house and Mrs Jones and the girls were fairly well 'with it', so life was a little bit different to the way that I had been brought up. I was young, as men go, just fifteen. I was treated as one of the family and as far as possible I shared most of the things that they had - for instance - when they entertained friends, it usually involved a dinner at night. Although I did not join them in the dining room I would be served exactly the same food at the same time, in the kitchen. Although I was fifteen years old I was only now to get my first experience of a bathroom. Up to now I had never seen one, leave alone been in one.

There was another person in the household during the week - that was believe it or not a Mr Lewis, the builder. He was building a new house on a plot of land bought from Mrs Jones and for the time that he was working on the house he stayed in the farm house. It would not be for long as the house was well under way before I came there. He was a rather special kind of 'one man band', as he was the only builder and had a kind of helper. Mr Lewis had apparently been to America to study the latest methods and he was I think, one of the first to do Artex interior decorating. This Artex was on the walls as well as the ceilings. When he was working on this he did it in secret - he would even cover up the windows, so that no one would see him working.

If you remember, the last mention we made of Ben and Dilys, we said that they had moved to Abergwilli. Abergwilli was not too far away from where I worked, so I would visit them frequently and by doing so, I met other lads that worked on farms, so I made some friends who were to be so for most of my time at Frongelly.

As I mentioned earlier, I was the only man, so, 'a man has to do what a man has to do'. Seriously, it meant that all the transporting of materials had to be done by horse and cart. So it meant that I made frequent trips to Carmarthen for cattle food etc.

Now the other reason for going to Carmarthen, was to attend the cattle mart which was a weekly event. There were occasions when calves were born on the farm and in most cases these would be sold at the mart, but some female calves were reared. Now, although I had done a lot of different things in my time, I had never taken a calf to the mart to be sold. I would take the calf in the cart to the mart, park the pony and cart, then I had to enter the calf and put it in a pen. I discovered that I had to get a kind of ticket, with a large number on it - this was not easy for me, as I had to jostle with other big, burly farmers. I managed this, but then had to go to another location, where I would find a big glue pot, on a heater. I had to put some of this on the ticket and run with it to put on the Calf, in the pen, before it cooled off. I as you can guess, went to the mart many times after that and became quite familiar with the routine.

In one section of the mart, where little piglets were sold, it was customary to take the pigs in the cart with a net over them, and leave them in a row with others, taking the horse out to the stable. The auctioneer would come along the row and sell each cart-full in turn. Now, as you probably know, there are many ways of making your bid known to the auctioneer - for instance - a nod of the head, or a wink but the most usual one is to raise your arm. Well, I was on this occasion, sitting on one of the unsold cartloads and I saw a mate of mine, not far away - I waved to him to attract his attention and the next thing I knew was the auctioneer asking 'what was my bid?' - I nearly got a cartload of pigs!

Frongelly was only about one or two miles from town, and although I did not go there very often in the evenings, I remember that it was about this time that I saw my first film in the cinema, it was Clark Gable and Jean Harlow in 'China Seas'. I got to like the cinema and I would go to the pictures whenever I could afford it. At that time it cost six old pence, downstairs, and twelve pence or one shilling upstairs, but when you consider that it took me more than a day to earn a shilling, it was expensive. Chocolate in those days was tuppence a bar, that was for a big bar, plain or Cadbury's fruit and nut. There was nothing I liked more than to take a bar of chocolate when I went to the pictures. There was something else that I liked equally and that was the stories in the comic called the 'Adventure'. Like today's comic stories it always closed on the most exciting time. I really enjoyed taking a bar of chocolate and the latest 'Adventure' to my room in the evening. I liked it especially, if it was raining - simple pleasures!

Now, one thing that I was well known for, was getting up early in the morning. This was important in a farmer's view, as a poor riser was less in demand, due to this fact. So this was very much in my favour. In my present situation I slept out in my bedroom and although I had no clock or watch, I used other means of telling the time. Frongelly was not only near the main road, but there was also a railway not far away and I remember that I got fairly familiar with the train times. There was the quarter to nine, the quarter to eleven and the twelve o'clock that told me it was dinner time, but I do not remember one to wake me up or to tell me the time to do so. Whatever it was that I used, I know there was no time-piece. I would just wake up, and that was the time to get up - or so it seems. However, there is, I suppose, usually an exception to everything. One morning I got up as usual; I fed the cows, and I started milking. Mrs Jones would usually join me at this time but this morning, alas, no Mrs Jones. It was not much longer before I realised that there was not much milk either. By now I was beginning to fear the worst, so I went outside the house and called to Mrs Jones. Then she popped her head out of the window -

her, first words were 'what is wrong?' What are you doing up at this time? - do you know the time?' 'It is only half past one!' Yes half past one! You can imagine how I felt.
Now, after this little episode I fixed up a bell on the bedroom wall (a cycle bell) with a string line across the yard to Mrs Jones' bedroom window. The plan was that she would endeavour to call me at getting up time but this did not work really, as I would wake up and think that the bell had not worked and with me 'up' and Mrs Jones pulling at the string, needless to say the plan fell through. It was then that Mrs Jones thought it worth spending some money on a watch for me (another first). I cannot really explain my feeling of delight. If you remember, when I was younger, my only wish in life was a bike and a watch - well now I was halfway there and after that we had no problems.

Time soon went by, and I had by now more or less been tested on all the aspects of work involved. Apart from the work at Frongelly, I had been to various places, as it was customary to help with threshing, haymaking, potato setting etc. These jobs I learnt at home, when I was younger. I must mention here that I was given advice by my father when I left home, and that was, if you do a job, make sure that you do it well, or don't do it at all. I can honestly say that I have abided by that rule, all through my life, and I still believe in it. Another bit of advice that I was given, when I was one day trimming the hedge alongside the road, and as usual tried very hard to complete as much as possible, and at the same time heeding my father's advice, so at the end I was quite pleased with my work. That evening I was talking to Tom Edwards, our neighbour, and we were on the road discussing my days work. I said that I had done from 'a' to 'b' which was quite a way. Now I was interested in his remark, he said, 'A lot of people will pass along this road, and with regard to the hedge, they would only look how it had been done, no one would wonder how long it took to complete!' Good sense I thought.

I had now completed my first year, and I had come to the end of my contract but we had re-negotiated my salary and I was now to get a rise of three pounds, bringing it to eighteen pounds per annum. So, I was on my way to year two, and about now I acquired an old bike, which needed a lot doing to it. This I did with some gusto! After a while I was able to ride it in the evenings to Abergwili to see my friends, and I would cycle through Carmarthen to Cwrt-y-Bedw. Father and mother were now left with only Audrey at home. Betty was working in Parcenthin Farm; Ben was in Abergwili and Mr Bowen the Moor, had been after Mary to work as a maid after she had been working in Nantego for about six months. Meanwhile, at Frongelly, the house that Mr Lewis the builder had built, was occupied by a family, which included a little girl of about five or six years of age. As the farm was so close she was allowed to come and see us nearly every day. Her parents were I believe 'town folk', certainly not Welsh. I remember my first contact with the lady of the house; she asked me if I would come and cut the lawns around the house as these were new, and the grass had got a bit long. So, one evening after work, along I went with a big scythe and a sickle and with all my practice, I was quite good! I finished the job and she paid me the sum of three shillings. That was really three days wages for me, so I was quite satisfied. However, after a little while the grass was in need of cutting again, but instead of asking for my services, the lady asked if she could borrow the cutting tools. Can you imagine her using the tools that I had used so effectively and probably made it look easy, however, I still ended up cutting the grass.

I had by now earned a year's salary and was able to buy a brand new bike - remember - the second item of my earlier dreams. I had then achieved, what seemed the ultimate. You could not possibly believe how happy it made me. I remember the first night out, I went over to Abergwili to show it off to my friends, as we all had bikes of a sort. My bike was a 'semi-drop handlebars', a Rally Sports and it cost four pounds nineteen shillings and sixpence. That was in wages, one hundred days work. It seemed that I had started something, as over a period of a few months, all the boys in our mob, and there were seven or eight of us altogether, bought a Rally Sports bike. I remember we would go round as a group, and when we called at a cafe or a shop, we would leave our bikes together, and as all were the same, it took some sorting out. It was now getting towards the summer, and the evening were sunny and long and I remember one of the boys, Harry, he actually came from Swansea and one Saturday or Sunday, he went home on his bike and in the evening, about seven o'clock, Arthur Francis and I decided we would go towards Swansea to meet Harry. Now Carmarthen, where we started from, was a distance of twenty seven miles from Swansea, that was one way. This really turned out to be a most memorable occasion. When we started out, we as young, fit lads, gave the idea little thought, even though this was after a days work, however, we went along the main road - not forgetting that we were looking for Harry coming to meet us. We went on and on and on, and eventually ended up in the streets of Swansea. We did not know where Harry lived, so there was only one thing left to do - yes - start the twenty seven miles back to Carmarthen! We were, to say the least, rather weary and did not make such good time as we did on the way up. The journey back became slower and slower, and I remember on several occasions we would stop, lie down on the wet grass on the roadside and then carry on. We eventually made it many hours after we had left at seven. It was now another day and I think that that was my first real lesson in cycling and I never forgot it.

I had, as a young boy, and up to now, enjoyed good health, and I had not lost any work days healthwise, but something strange happened to me. One day I noticed that I had a kind of a round red ring, on the back of my hand. This did not bother me much at the time, but as the days went by it grew bigger in circumference 'and there were more' - yes there were more little ones. These got bigger and more numerous, until I really had to take notice. They were I thought ringworm, so I went to see a doctor, I say a doctor as I had not been before. He confirmed the fact that it was ringworm, and gave me some ointment to put on it. Well as time went by, these things multiplied, and grew to an alarming state, so my journey to the doctor got more and more frequent and then I was told by someone, I forget who, that a chemist in town had a cure for ringworm. By now I was on the sick, but still at Frongelly. In desperation I went to see the chemist. Now, it seemed that the treatment that he had was a secret, so you had to be treated by him, in the shop premises. After the first lot of treatment (which by the way was a liquid that he painted on) although it hurt, it seemed to do some good. By now the ring/patches had spread all over my body, with one on each shoulder the size of saucers. I was still visiting the doctor, but he did not know of my other treatment. On one visit, he said 'to keep treating it with the ointment - his! The climax came for me after one of my visits to the chemist. I felt afterwards as if my skin was cracking. I could not go to bed, I could not even sit down - I stood up all night in my bedroom without any clothes on. After that things improved immensely and I did not need to go for any more treatment - that was my salvation - by the way, that chemist shop is still there to this day, and I think it is kept by the same family.

By now I was into my second year at Frongelly, and I felt quite an established farm worker. I got on well with Mrs Jones, but I can remember one or two occasions when our true Welsh spirits clashed, but we always sorted things out in the end. Mrs Jones had a car and she used to get around - I say 'around' because there was one thing that she could not do, turn the car round -well maybe in a round about way! She could not reverse it. We usually ended up pushing it in and out of the garage - there was no driving test in those days.

Farming people did not necessarily get an annual holiday. This was definitely true as the workers were concerned, as when you were hired, you were hired for three hundred and sixty fives days, but practically you could ask for an occasional day off. Now, Mrs Jones did have a holiday each year. She would, as far as I remember, go to Aberystwyth for two weeks. This left Phillys and myself to look after the work on the farm. I think that by now I had experienced most of the things that happened on such a farm.

I mentioned earlier that I had had my first experience of a bathroom at Frongelly, although my visits to the bathroom were not so frequent. My washing and shaving were performed in the horse trough, in cold water, this seemed quite reasonable at the time; oh, I must not forget cleaning my teeth in the same trough but under the cold water tap.

My friend Arthur Francis, from Abergwili, had left his farm job and had joined the RAF. Now, when he came home on his first leave, we were all rather impressed with him and I think that this was the very first time I thought of joining the RAF. I have thought of my situation at that age, literally starting out in life, and although I was quite happy doing farm work, you begin to wonder, 'Is this what I should be doing?' The answer always seemed to be the same - I cannot afford not to do it. So this narrowed the choice. I was to ask myself this question many more times in my young life.

I have not mentioned religion since I left home, well I did not want to or indeed could not let this go. So when I first came to Frongelly, I discovered on my visits to my brother at Abergwili, that he was a regular attender at the Congregational Chapel, which was on the other side of the road from his house; so I was introduced in this way and not long afterwards I was made a member and attended not regularly, but kept in touch - this of course pleased my father and mother.

Time soon went by and I was now nearly seventeen years old and I was coming to the end of my second year with Mrs Jones but I was to stay for yet another year, with a new agreed salary of twenty five pounds. The third year went by with not much difference except of course that I was growing up. In fact, little did I know, that I was grown up enough to fill one of the places on Mr Bowen The Moor's farm. He now asked me if I would come and work for him. Now this was, I suppose, in a way, promotion and the money would be much more. Well, if you remember, it had always been my ambition to work at The Moor, just a small field away from my childhood home, Broad Moor. This of course was not a decision that I would take without consulting my father and mother, more from the point of respect I suppose, it seemed that I still belonged to them, however it was more or less a forgone conclusion and I left Frongelly, a place that I had lived in for - yes - three important years and 'my first job'. You do not live with people without getting attached to them to a certain extent. So it was not altogether a happy occasion when Mr Bowen arrived to collect my box. Little did I know at the time, that I had stayed in Frongelly one year longer than the time originally agreed between Mr Bowen and Mrs Jones. It appeared that the agreement was, that I would be in Frongelly until I was seventeen, old enough to work at the Moor - the reason was that Mrs Jones would not release me.

No mention has yet been made of clothes worn on farms in those days. It was customary to obtain certain items for winter and naturally different types for summer. The items for winter were - breeches and leggings, flannel shirts, leather boots, with hob-nails to cover the sole. A jacket would be worn most of the time - note - no mention of vests. This was due to the superb, absorbing qualities of the thick woollen shirt. Now, this kit would be far too warm in summer, so the cord breeches would be replaced by cord trousers, but it was considered that the thick woollen shirts, were as effective in absorbing the sweat and grime in the summer, as it was at keeping you warm in the winter. The jackets were not really necessary but a light denim type could be used. An alternative to the trousers could be dungarees, bib and brace.

So it was that I was to arrive in my new work-place, with mostly new kit. This would now be October, with the winter not too far ahead. By this time, Mary, my sister, had just completed her first year at the

Moor. Although we were to work in the same place, our jobs were poles apart. I mentioned previously the custom of sleeping 'out' or sleeping 'in'. Well, here I was to sleep in the house, in a bedroom above the kitchen. This did not really make much difference except of course, if you slept in, arrangements had to be made for the nights when you came in late, after a night out and of course your movements were known as they had to leave the door unlocked.

Work at the Moor was to be a lot different from Frongelly except the daily routine, husbandry of animals, and of course, the other main factor was that there would be two of us. This included Mr Bowen. I previously mentioned two labourers at the Moor, but this was before Mr Bowen came. My work was a mixture of two aspects of farming, cows and horses. My interest was mainly in the horses and the work in the fields but I soon found out that here at least, the other aspects of work had to be done as well. One job that I had not encountered before was my involvement with a bull. This was in the days before artificial insemination, when most farms with a reasonable sized herd of cows kept a bull. There are like all animals different breeds - for beef - a Hereford bull, which are by nature, rather quiet and timid, while the dairy bull, like Friesian or Shorthorn are usually quite fierce. My experience started on the first morning, when I was informed that it was usual to let the bull out of the 'loose box' to the small field close by. I should have realised when I saw the pitch fork outside the loose box door, but how was I know that this was the fiercest bull in the district. What happened when I opened the door left me rooted to the spot as I saw this massive hulk of a bull came flying past me and go to the gate which I would have opened, to allow it to go into the field. When the bull reached the gate it proved to be no obstruction as it lowered its head and charged the full sized gate and took it part way into the field. This then was the animal that I had come to live with, as it would be my job each morning to let him out. Now if this was a problem, it was simple compared with fetching the bull back from the field, especially as it did not want to return to its box. I had

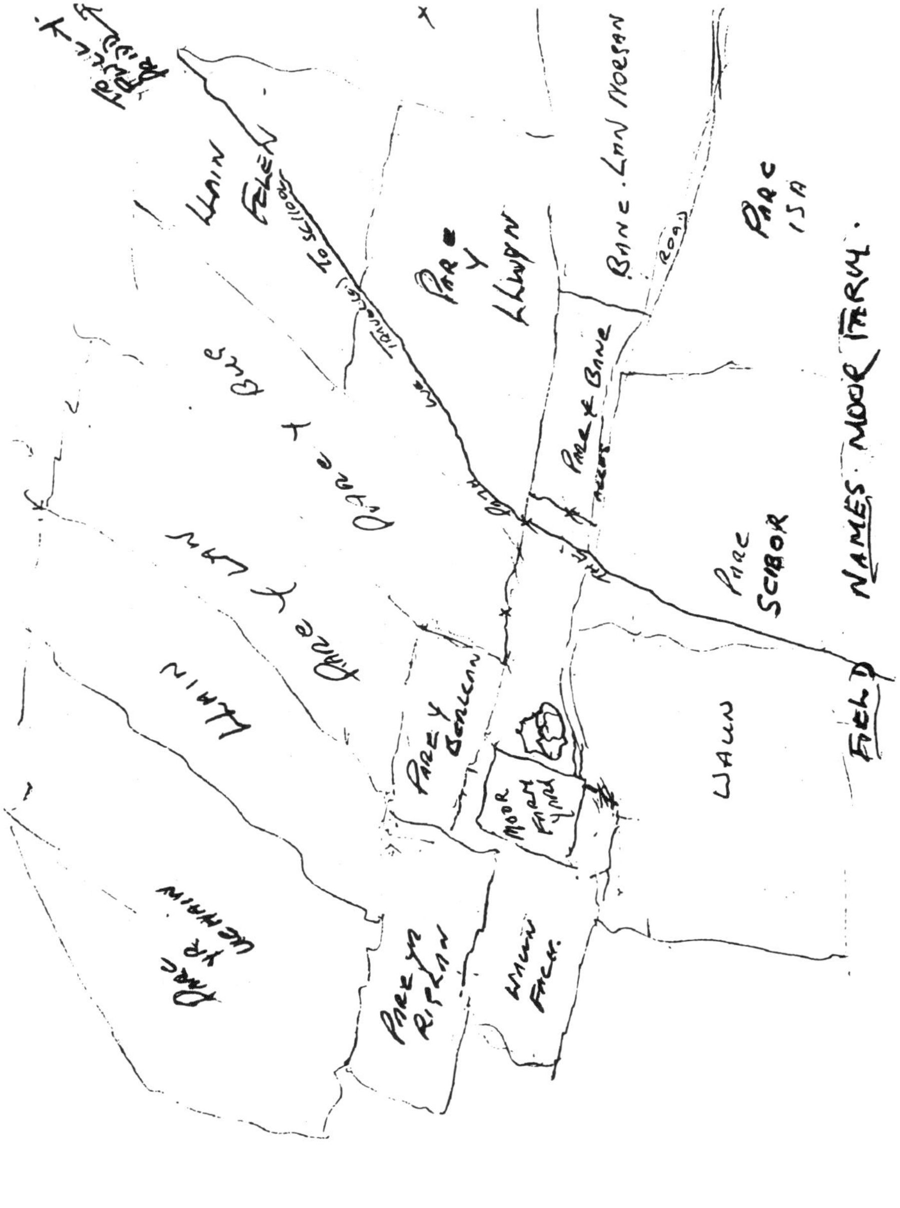
NAMES. MOOR FARM. FIELD
PARC ISA
PARC SCIBOR
WAUN
MOOR FARM YARD
PARC Y LLWYN
ROAD
TO SCHOOL

never been afraid of any animal up to now, except maybe the sow that chased my father but that was easily overcome. I was not really afraid now – maybe it would have been better if I had been. However, I went with pitch fork in hand, and this gave me some confidence. I got out to the middle of the field and I was immediately charged by this mad animal, head down, as if he was going to treat me the same as the field gate. Then, and only then, did I realise that I could be fighting for my life, there was no escape. If I had run, he would have attacked me from behind, so I had to face him with the pitch fork. I remember hitting him over the eyes many times and I thought that I was winning, but he kept on coming with his eyes closed, his head near the ground; my defence up to now was hitting out with the fork, but I then realised that I was trying to prod him with the point of the fork. A bull's forehead is like a brick wall, so I went for the softer parts and I then saw blood coming from somewhere, it was his nose. Now, this could have made things worse for me, but fortunately it did not and this was when I thought I was winning and I think the bull agreed and he started to retreat, suddenly turned around and made for the gateway. That was my first encounter of many but I was never to be surprised again and I think, that as a result of our encounter the bull had a little respect for me, but I could not depend on it. I mentioned earlier in my story about my wish to join the RAF but after this little episode I thought of trying for a job in Spain!

I think that it is appropriate to mention here another incident which occurred several years earlier at The Moor; it was during my early days when I would go to help out. I was about the time when Mr Bowen arrived and married Polly. Her sister had also got married and had gone away. So, it was that the farm stock and other items of farm implements were divided up. I well remember a lorry load of various items and a bull - not the same one - which was loaded on as the last item. Unfortunately, when the lorry started moving out over the rough yard, the poor bull was thrown off balance and as it was tied to the lorry by the ring in its nose, the ring was pulled through, causing it to tear and as a result spent the next half hour trying to get out; 'enough bull'.

I was now back in my old home area and I was not the only one - that had grown up. All my school mates from around, like David John and Gwilym, his brother, were working on farms. Some of the girls had now blossomed into young women and Oswald had joined the RAF. He never really had a happy home life. He was different - he was clever at school, and preferred learning to working. Oswald was a one parent child. Now, this was not common in those days and was looked on as being 'wrong'. When he was about thirteen or fourteen, his mother Jane married a man named Johnny Morris. You remember, he was one of our daily visitors when we lived in Broad Moor. Somehow Oswald was not his kind, and they did not get on. Just before joining the RAF Oswald lived with his Aunty Sarah, Morfa Bach while his mother and Johnny lived in Bronhaul. I cannot remember exactly when, but not long after I arrived at The Moor, one Sunday morning, we heard the terrible news that Oswald had been killed in an aircraft crash. He would be far too young, to be part of any aircrew. Apparently, he and another lad, went for a flip, as they called it, with a pilot who was taking an aircraft on test. It appears they came down over the sea at Felixstowe and were never seen again.

Every day life and work at the Moor was very different from Frongelly, mainly because the Moor was a bigger farm and therefore did grow a lot of animal fodder, such as - corn, mangolds, turnips and of course, potatoes. So it was about now, that these crops would be gathered in before the frost. In spite of all this, this was a dairy farm, like most farms in this part of Wales. They used to say - that you were judged by the size of your monthly milk cheque. Milking was a job that had to be done twice each day 'come what may'. We had not yet got to the milking machine days, so, at the appropriate time six thirty in the morning and about five in the evening, the 'boss' as he was referred to, the 'Missus' his wife, my sister Mary and myself, would be involved in milking about twenty cows. Now milking by hand is not easy, and it takes time. We would all start in the same shed, as there were several, and progress from cow to cow. Some cows were easier to milk than others and some could be really tough, and you can imagine the jockeying for positions to try and miss the really tough ones. Milking was one of the last jobs of the day, after which we would all clean up and go into the house, to 'sit' I suppose. This was the end of the working day, but there was one more little chore to be done before retiring and that was after supper, we had to go out to bed the cows down. So when you were all relaxed and ready for bed, the boss would light the hurricane lamps, one to each shed. Incidentally, the boss was said to be mean, he would only use one match to light all the lamps. If it was necessary he would use 'dead' matches to light one from the other. So, out we would go, sometimes into the cold, maybe wet, but once in the cowshed, it was usually warm. There was always a certain smell when hay or bedding was shaken, the dust would burn in the hurricanes.

There was one day when the milking was usually done in record time - Saturday. This was so that Mary and myself could catch the bus to town for our weekly night out. Most of my travelling was done by bike. I would go out once or twice in the winter, usually once a week to Cwrt-y-Bedw, to see mother and father. I suppose I was a little nearer than I was in Frongelly. They were always pleased to see me, especially mother - God bless her. My visit was usually after a hard days work in the fresh air and after supper we would sit around the fire and I would sometimes fall asleep. This could be for some considerable time but my mother would always wait until I woke up, she would never disturb me, she would sometimes wait for an hour or more.

The part of my work that I enjoyed the most was when I worked with horses. I had several of the largest shire horses and apart from looking after them I would also spend a lot of my time out in the fields doing numerous jobs. As this was just before the tractor era, all the work had to be done with horses, from carting out the cow - muck from the yard to ploughing the fields. Now this was a task that I had never had the opportunity to do but I was not to be denied, this came first of all at the Witil, remember the shares, like father had, Mr Bowen had one as well. The most difficult part of ploughing is the start and the finish. To start you have to drive two horses, hold the plough and, hold a straight course across the field. For the first time Mr Bowen did this and then I carried on. He left me to sort it out and I must have done well as he would not believe that it was my first attempt.

Having read this far, you may say that there are no funny bits in this story. Well, if I said that it was not a 'funny farm' that should raise a chuckle! Farm work tends to be rather serious as you spend a lot of time working alone or at best, with animals and they do not appreciate jokes, if that raised a chuckle then this chapter should possibly raise a laugh. It was early one morning and we found one of the cows needed the attention of our famous bull. I let the cow out to the yard and opened the loose box door as usual, out came the 'beast' and for once he did not try to escape as his interest was in another direction - the cow, but the cow did not seem to like the idea. It became very frightened and was looking for an escape from this beastly bull!

Just about this time, the boss was in the course of taking the van through the yard gate to take the milk to the factory. Now, whether the cow or the bull saw it first, I do not know, as both made a dash for the gateway. Meantime the boss seeing this happen, jumped into the van and tried to get away. At the same time the bull focused its attention on the moving van, the boss realising the situation, was trying to pick up speed, but with a load of full milk churns, and driving up the hill, he was not making much headway, but the bull, with his head down and his tail up, was gaining and was aiming straight at the rear doors of the van. I think the cow, in its fright, beat both the van and the bull, and just as the 'circus' came opposite another open gate, both animals disappeared into the open field. The bull's interest had now it seemed, switched back in the appropriate direction. This was now a 'free for all'. Meanwhile I could see my job of rounding up this lot, getting more difficult by the minute (and there's more). They went across the field and the cow ended up lying down in a pond and the bull astride. We were very near my old home Broadmoor and Cliff Roberts came to help me, and between us we drove the bull into a corner and I was able to get a piece of rope into the ring in its nose, and we travelled back to the yard a lot tidier than when we came out.

The winter months 'saw you' out in the fields, doing the various jobs, like thrashing, ditching, cutting hedges, spreading cow muck. This was hard work, I had done a lot of this from the time at home in Cwrt-y-Bedw, but here it was a far bigger job and although muck spreading was not my favourite job. I have always been blessed with being interested in any job that I am involved with and I have carried this ability with me even up to this day. I worked hard, and I would set myself a target and I cannot remember ever failing to achieve it. I liked to think that I set a kind of 'record breaker', remember in Frongelly it was hedge cutting, well here it was muck spreading. I would strive to get an early start, which I did this day, once started I would work every minute and by the end of the day, I had done so much that when the boss told me next morning to continue with what I was doing yesterday, I was able to say that I had finished.

Occasionally I would get the opportunity to get off the farm, like the horse sales I went to. I remember taking horses to Llanybyther, which was a long way away and would take all day. Believe it or not, I would walk all the way, leading the horse and when I got there it would take a long time to sell. You would 'run' your horse, up and down the road for each prospective buyer.

With the winter now over, the spring was always welcome, when the cows, would go out to sleep at night and the evenings lengthened -

the grass would grow and everything improved. I liked the long light evenings when I was 'not out'. I would take the gun out and roam around the fields, shooting rabbit and wood pigeons, which I would take back for the pot. Rabbits in those days were considered to be good value, as myxomatosis had not yet arrived - so a rabbit - a good piece of bacon, from the stock, usually hanging in the kitchen -a nice green cabbage from the garden, along with carrots, swedes, leeks and potatoes, would make a good meal and of course produced the good old 'cawl', the Welsh broth.

In the 'bull' episode, you may realise that I mentioned Mr Bowen, taking milk to the factory in a van, well yes, things had progressed a lot in the last year or two, since my pony and cart days, and farmer's vans were one of the first considerations, as these could be used to take stock to the market etc. etc.

It appears that being that the vans were used for business purposes the tax would be reduced. However, you can imagine the numerous occasions, when these would be required for personal use - for instance - to take us to chapel in St Clears on a Sunday and although, in fact, that kind of journey was not in the category of business, so to get around that Mr Bowen would catch a chicken, tie its legs together, and put it in the back of the van. When he returned home, the chicken was released and all was back to normal - problem solved. I should mention here, that if he'd been asked the reason for his journey, I am sure he would have thought of a friend in St Clears, that he would be delivering the chicken to.

Spring soon came and went and all that is associated with it. All the seed corn had been set, all the hay fields had been treated, and it is a glorious time watching things grow. Before you know it you are in the summer. This brings hay-making and later corn harvesting with the exceptionally long working day. It was not unusual to finish one day at eleven o'clock at night, release the poor hardworking horses

Ploughing

Mowing

PROPORTIONAL PARTICIPATION

There were many combinations of horsepower to accommodate all the various aspects of farming. Depending on the requirement, horses were used singularly - in tandem or even in teams of three. Wherever more than one horse was involved, a system of whippletrees was used to ensure a fair distribution of the work.

Where two horses were involved each horse was attached, one either side of the pivot point, ensuring a balanced result. Where three horses were used side-by-side as a team, it became a bit more complicated to ensure equal effort from all three. For instance, the horse in the center could vary its effort un-noticed, placing a greater load on the other two horses. To eliminate this possibility a system of whippletrees was used to attach the load.
The proportional division of the long sharing beam in this horizontal see-saw results in horse number 1 having the advantage of the leverage against horses 2 and 3 on the short side, resulting in balance and equal effort. Not only is the single horse balanced against the other two, the other two are balanced against each other, as in pairs.

Whippletrees:- Distribution of workload

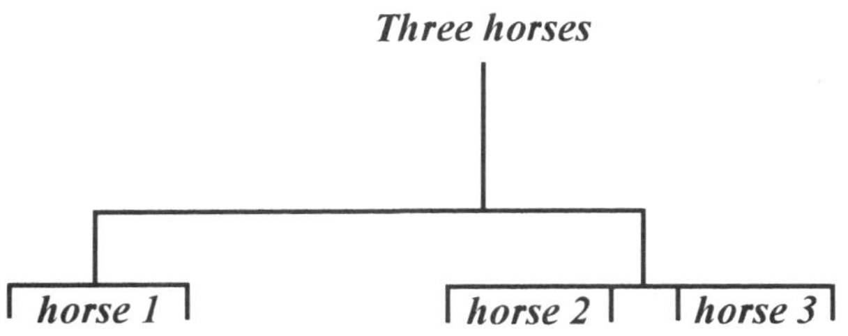

PROCLAMATION

This is a proclamation of a feat of magnificent achievement performed by:-

WILLIAM WYNDHAM LEWIS

On a day in the autumn of the year, one thousand, nine hundred and thirty nine, in the process of his daily duties and by virtue of his sheer strength, will and determination - and without assistance from any kind of mechanical object, successfully completed a self-set task of spreading and causing the surface of this pasture to be covered with 'dung' - this being the end product of the creatures of the yard.

The above being set out in three rows - in heaps of a size and quantity to be the equivalent of seven heaps per cart-load - set seven steps apart - and seven steps between each stepped row of approximately seven hundred yards.

He in so doing, it is believed set a world record that should be of interest to persons of equivalent ambition. Therefore this is hereby proclaimed to be

A RECORD OF ACHIEVEMENT

Should any person as a result of reading this proclamation wish to challenge this magnificent feat of work, let him now speak or forever hold his peace.

Signed by ....
W W LEWIS

This proclamation is just an enhancement of a down-to-earth and simple job known as 'MUCK SPREADING' but it is considered by this human muck spreader to be a record.

PLOUGHING SHIRES

Way back in olden days
We tilled the land in different ways.
We used the Shires and their power –
They did it all, though maybe slower.

It now seems long ago and far away
Since we tilled the fields in this way,
Ploughing, harrowing and sowing the seed,
All of it done with those trusty old steeds.

In those days when we worked on the land
With Shires in excess of twenty hands,
They worked in pairs and sometimes three,
Obeying instructions – silently.

We wandered lonely, up and down,
With no interference – not a sound.
Those big, quiet giants, with their silent might,
Straining to keep those tethers tight.

We crossed the field, to and fro,
Cutting a furrow as we go,
Turning it over and upside down,
Changing its colour from green to brown.

This was the time that the tractor appeared
Far more substantial and yes, higher geared.
It could do more in an hour, dare I say,
Than we did with horses in a full working day.

Cont/

Maybe horses tire at the end of the day,
Tractors, of course – not affected this way.
Tractors are unfriendly, not like the horse,
Although you can ride and have shelter of course.

Now that the tractor has actually arrived,
Those Shires could not have really survived.
As those tractors became more abundant
The trustry old steeds were soon made redundant.

It was all in the name of progress, they say.
True, the old tractor does not eat any hay
But this was the beginning that signalled the end
Of that magnificent creature – man's best friend.

---

from their harnesses and go to supper. At this time of the year the mares have young foals and during the long working day they are separated, you can imagine the reunion at about this time, it is supper time for them as well! I have on some occasions been up at three o'clock to harness the horses again and go out to mow another field of hay. The reason for this unearthly hour was that mowing hay was a very hard, hot job, and we would try and get as much done as possible, before the sun got too high in the sky, and an added bonus, I suppose, for the boss was that we still had most of the day left to work on other hay-fields which were probably ready for harvesting.

During the very busy time of the year, Mr Bowen would hire a kind of casual labourer, ha, casual he was, but labourer I don't know, but he was fun! His name was Stanley, aged about fifty - ancient in those days. Remember I mentioned earlier that we did not have much fun working on the farm, well, when Stan, as we called him was around, he was a laugh. Sometimes, in the presence of the boss and missus, when we looked at each other, we went into laughs, for no apparent reason, probably on reflection of some funny incident earlier on.

There was I suppose, an added bonus to the job, apart from the pay and the food and that was the ' home brew'. It was customery for farmers to brew large quanties of beer for consumption by the workers during the harvest period. Stan liked his beer, especially free beer! It was strange when you think of it, one could drink beer during the hot day and hardly be affected by it, I suppose it was the fact that you sweat it out. The people that really liked beer would have more when they finished work.

Now Stan worked on a daily basis and he travelled daily on his bike from Laugharne – there were no breathalysers in those days! I remember on one occasion walking down the farm road with Stan – it would be eleven or twelve midnight – and dark. He had no cycle light, well no battery in his lamp and when we discussing the problem, Stan in his funny way, put his bike down by the hedge and was collecting something from the hedge. When I asked him what he was trying to do, he said ' If I have a few of these in my lamp I will be OK' I then realised he was picking up glow-worms, 'big laugh', strangely enough the hedge along the lane was covered with the fluorescent effect. In spite of these long late, working hours, I could still wake up each morning at the exact time that I had set. After three or four hours sleep, I would wake up without any problem, this was I suppose, a special gift that I possessed and believe it or not I enjoyed it.
After the hay-harvest is over, you will see most farms in Wales with the hay barns/hay sheds full. There are very few farms without these hay barns. It is or was very important that the hay should be 'fit' before it is harvested. That means weathered, from the green stage and also dry, otherwise when it was put into the hay sheds, it would develop heat and could even go on fire. This did not happen very often but sometimes, when the hay was cut for use in the winter, if it

had not been properly harvested, it would be dark brown or even black

One day not long after most farms had finished the harvest, I was working in the field, on a nice, sunny, warm day and what I saw I could not believe - looking across some fields, I could see clearly the hay barn of Creswell Farm and as I watched, I could see flames and smoke, coming from one side. I realised that the whole hay barn was on fire. I ran immediately to our farm yard to tell them and then across the fields to the fire. It would be about two o'clock in the afternoon when it started and by the time I got there, many of the neighbours had arrived. The fire had really taken hold and there was not much one could do. The fire engine soon arrived (no, it was not horse drawn!) but having got there, there was no source of water to tap. The firemen used what water they had and then set about protecting the surrounding buildings, including the house. We did what we could, but then they decided that the fire was not likely to reach the house. I, along with others, stayed most of the day and into the night, as the hay would just smoulder and take a long time to burn out. Later, when it was safe to do so, we started throwing the mass of partly burned hay out and spreading it. This took a long time. I cannot remember when I got back to the Moor, but I could remember that I was black and very tired. The following day I could hardly walk as my legs were so stiff from treading in the burned hay. I cannot remember what day the fire occurred but what I do recollect, is that Sunday soon came and as it was the only day when I had some free time I went up to the hay - loft and put my legs on the wall and went to sleep in the hay. This did help an awful lot. No one discovered how the fire started, some said that a young boy was playing with matches but do we know?

The corn harvest follows on soon after hay making and this for me was a new experience. This of course was before combine harvesters and as it was done with horses it involved me very much. This operation required more people because women were involved stacking the sheaves as the binder went around and around the field, and finished in the middle. This was often quite exciting as all the rabbits in the corn field, ended up in the last little bit, and we often tried to catch them. Some times, a few dogs would take part and you could use a gun if you were careful. When we talk about the hay and the corn harvest, the other menial jobs, like milking and caring for the animals, have to be done by someone and maybe we have not made much mention of the women of the farm. They had to work very hard, to carry on the milking etc. This is as well as making food for the people involved in the harvesting.

About this time of year, on the farm, you can sometimes find mushrooms in the fields. Now, I have always been fond of these and had found out that Mr Bowen was very partial to them. So, in the free evenings, I would go and look for mushrooms and we would have them for supper. On one of these expeditions I found some mushrooms but not sufficient for all of us for a meal. So, on my return I handed them over to the misses and remarked 'that there were not too many, so it was not much use sharing them out, just a good meal for one person' because I realised how much the boss like them. When supper was ready, we sat on the long table together and the plate of mushrooms was given to me - can you imagine my horror - Mrs Bowen had mistaken my remark to mean that there was only enough for me, and the worst part of all was that I was too embarrassed to do anything about it. They must have thought that I was greedy, after all the mushrooms came from their land. I know now what I should have done but at that age I could not cope with the situation.

In my ambitious way I would always try to do things as fast as possible, for instance, cleaning out the cowshed, after the cows went back to the field, but, I thought it would be better still if it did not have to be done at all. To this end, I started to prevent the cows doing their jobs' in the sheds and believe it or not, in a short period of time, I managed to achieve this strange objective. This meant that when the cows went out of their sheds to the yard, they did what they should have done inside - outside! For a while I accepted this but before long I started preventing this happening, even in the yard. Result - I had the keenest herd of cows to reach the field. Mr Bowen was a very keen man himself and when he realised my aim, he was as keen as I was - there's more - all others tried to help in this strange operation, result - not only did it prevent the sheds and the yards being mucked on, but it actually transported the cow muck to the fields.

I do not know really, whether this story has any connection with that exercise; it happened one day, when I had the occasion to take one of the cows through some fields, and I was leading it by the halter. I do not remember exactly where it should have gone to, but what happened next had some effect on that. I opened the gate into the field, took the cow through and I then used one hand to hold the cow, while closed the gate with the other. Now, for whatever reason, the cow saw its chance and bolted. This took me completely off balance and I ended up on my stomach on the ground and it was in this position that I was to be towed at speed across the field. The rope halter, I discovered later was around one finger only - I have a mark to this day! Now, what I did not bargain for, was that as I was dragged along on my stomach, to my horror I could see cow pats coming towards me, or so it seemed - that was one cow-pat that would have been better in the yard. It was me that was moving though, and at such speed, that when I eventually stopped, a fair amount of the cow-pats had been forced into my trouser top, and beyond (not a pretty sight). We were both still together when I stopped - the cow and I!

You may wonder by now, how I had enough time for all this to happen to me. Well, by now, fairly well to form, I had agreed to stay for another year with Mr Bowen, and as one year seems very much the same as the next, it is difficult to date all these occasions. You may also be wondering what happened to my enemy - the bull - well, wonder no more, as I shall endeavour to relate yet another of his escapades. This, as most others happened was when it was let out in the morning. The reason for his outings was so that I could enter the loose box to clean it out and take his food in. While I was involved in this, I heard someone shouting in the distance - I went to investigate and found out that James - Moor Outlet, the small adjoining farmer, shouting to attract my attention, that the bull had found its way into his field, and was causing havoc amongst his cows. As usual I grabbed my lethal weapon - my pitchfork, went through a gate to James' field. Now James would not help me as he was not familiar with bulls. However, in my usual way I persuaded the bull to go in the direction of the open gate, got him through and I turned around to close the gate and immediately realised what I had done, I had presented my back to the bull, I had dropped my guard and I saw once more this creature with head down, heading straight for me. Although I had my pitchfork at the time I had it with it points upwards, with my thumb in the middle like a staff, therefore, all that I could do had to be done with the blunt end and so I was once more fighting this beast in earnest. The result, believe it or not, could be very serious for me. I urgently hit with the handle of the pitchfork, and continued to hit the bull's eyes on both sides until he had to travel backwards and I kept reversing him until I was opposite the gate. I ran into the yard but the bull was now right behind me and would probably have caught up with me had I not reached the steps leading to the store loft. I went to the top of the steps, while the bull, claiming a victory I suppose, was pawing the ground with his hoof but I was safe after yet another close encounter.

While all these fights were happening, you may wonder, as I did, what the boss was doing about this dangerous problem. In my position, I could not really complain, as this could be mistaken for a sign of weakness and I could not have that! It was a case of 'who's afraid of the big bad bull?' However, one day when the boss returned from his trip to the milk factory, he said to me, 'Come and see what I have brought.' He had a dog - a kind of a sheep dog I suppose. Maybe it looked a bit mean for that purpose, come to think of it. He explained that he had been given it by another farmer, who was glad to be rid of it. Apparently, it was intended to help with cows and sheep but it was so fierce that it was a danger to animals of any kind. It was called 'Gilo'. Now that name came to mean a lot to me, but much more to the bull. When I tried the dog out on the bull next morning, I let it go into the field where the bull was and the dog made a dash for the bull. The bull, as usual lowered his head for an attack, but the dog went for the other end. The bull took off with Gilo in pursuit, and round the field they went, and eventually the bull made for the yard and the sanctuary of his loose box. Needless to say that was the end of my involuntary confrontation with the bull. After a while I did not even have to produce Gilo, it was enough to call his name and the bull would come running in - what a relief! Was I pleased? Well, at that age you somehow appreciate a challenge and now that this had gone forever, a bit sorry I suppose. Now I do know someone who was very pleased, and that was my mother, who used to worry and each time I went home she used to tell me 'to be careful of that old bull'.

You would think that now the bull problem had been solved, life would be simpler and quieter, well, where you have animals, life is never dull. My next incident concerned horses, which if you remember, were my main job and my main interest. The horses on most farms were big shires and the ones I had were some of the biggest and were young, four or five year olds. Life for them was spent, mostly on the farm, except for the rare occasions when it was necessary to take them to the blacksmiths for shoeing. Well it was on one of these excursions that I was to experience another 'first'.

The horse concerned was called Diamond, a very lively mare - it was in the shafts of a 'Gambo' a long kind of cart, in which I would be riding, and I had also in the 'Gambo' a horse drawn plough, which was being taken to the blacksmiths for repair. Now, the road that I was travelling was the main road to St Clears, the same route as I travelled in my milk carting days, when I was small. But, this now seemed so long ago and so far away from my little pony, to this great big 'shire' that I was controlling. Although the horse was nervous of traffic, our journey to St Clears was without incident and so we arrived outside old George Brown's Blacksmiths shop.

What happened next, took me completely by surprise. I dismounted and was standing by the shop door, talking to the smithy and as I stood there, I saw, coming down the street, what was a common sight in those days, a Gypsy pony and flat cart, the kind that they used to collect rags and bones in. The Gypsy was going from door to door, leaving the leading of the pony to the little boy, yes, quite a small boy. At that moment he was trying to stop the pony, but I think, as it was coming straight for my horse, it did not want to stop. Realising the situation I ran the short distance to help him, but, just as I reached him, I heard something behind me and when I turned again, I was horrified to see my horse turn around to go back down the main street, towards home. Now, just as it was completing the turn, I managed to grab the shafts of the cart and I was I suppose, carried along with my feet hardly touching the floor, by now the horse, in its fright, was developing a real old gallop. I was gradually able to reach the reins that were dangling from its head, which was held high in its effort to increase speed. I hung on, and by now, this hunk of might and muscle was galloping down the main street, on its way home. However, I managed to gradually slow it down and as we went I saw people who were trying to stay out in the middle of the road, trying to help me. But, as we approached, they had to jump for safety. I did eventually, by shouting, and jarring at the bit, managed to stop and turn it around and once more get to the blacksmiths. I dread to think what would have happened had I failed to stop Diamond, it would have probably arrived home without me or it could have come to a sticky end and I don't suppose I could have ever lived that down.

During my early days with horses, I remember there was a lot of horse traffic on the roads – this was, in the main, farming traffic, taking the milk to the factory and returning with the necessary items such as animal food etc. Few people would realize that the horse, in addition to hauling the heavy cart loads, were equally involved holding back the same when negotiating steep hills. This applied especially in Wales as these are in places quite steep.

Some horse drawn traps and spring carts were equipped with brakes but heavier carts and gambos were not, even though these were heavier. There was however in my early days, a gadget called a drag or sled – in Welsh – llysc. These were used in most extreme cases to immobilise one wheel. The wheels were constructed of wood and metal in those days. The drag which was made entirely of heavy metal, was shaped to cradle the cartwheel, just the part in contact with the road. The drag was attached by a heavy linked chain of a specific length and attached to a position forward of the wheel, usually the base of the shaft. When not in use it would hang from a hook close to its anchor. When required for use at the top of a steep hill, it would be placed on the road immediately in front of the wheel. The wheel would mount the drag, the chain would tighten. The wheel would then be immobilised. At the bottom of the hill when no longer required, it would be stowed away.

Farming was an every day and all year round job, in all kinds of weather, so the horse had to travel regardless of conditions. The horses with metal shoes experienced difficulty while travelling on the tarred surface of the road, especially in frosty conditions. In such circumstances it was customery to call at the 'smithy' to insert special 'frost nails' in the horse shoes – normally two per shoe. These would replace normal nails. The frost nails had wedge shaped heads and would protrude further, to grip the road in frosty weather. These I suppose would give the horse some confidence. When conditions reverted to normal the nails would be removed.

Horses were of course used in other ways. Horse were used as a mode of transport to carry people around the countryside in the course of their work and leisure. A typical example of this would be the local vicar who would probably be provided with a horse for the visiting of his parishioners.

If I may I would like to deviate from the 'actual' and briefly enter the realms of ' fantasy' with a tale of the shoeing of the vicar's horse. The story goes that the vicar sent his young curate with the horse, to the blacksmith, to have the horse 'shod'. The curate was given strict instructions not to pay the 'asking' price but to bargain with the smithy for a reduced rate. The curate, keen to prove his abiltiy to deal with the task set him by the vicar, enquired the cost of the shoeing. When informed of the cost, the curate appeared very shocked and told the smithy in strong terms (within his profession) that it was too much. The smithy appeared to relent and came up with an alternative – cheaper – or so it seemed to the poor unsuspecting curate, who immediately agreed. The smithy's terms were – he would charge one halfpenny for the first nail in the shoe and then for each succeeding nail the cost would be double the cost of the preceeding one, so the second nail would cost one penny and the third, two pennies and so on. There were six nails per shoe with four shoes – making a total of twenty four nails. The cost would eventually be a very surprising total to a very surprised and sorry vicar. This placed him in a bit of a predicament – did he pay? Being a man of the cloth – we assume a man of his word!

There was, of course, a lot of normal farm work to be done and I was by now approaching the end of my second year at the Moor. Since I left Frongelly, nearly two years ago, I still had the thought of joining the RAF and about now I was thinking more and more about it. Actually, when Mr Bowen tried to get me to stay for another year I told him I was going to join the RAF and although he tried many times to persuade me to stay, he eventually went and hired someone else - George.

Now, there were two Hiring Fair times, and although you did not always get hired during the autumn fairs, you still used the dates to start and end your year. The first date, 12th October, and the other was the 14th November. I was due to leave the Moor on the 14th November, but Mr Bowen hired George from the 12th October, so for a brief period four or five weeks, we were to be there together. I think there could have been an ulterior motive here, for George to pick up the routine from me before I left.

During this time, my RAF idea was not developing as it was 1938/1939 just before the war and it turned out that farming people were not included in the conscription as they were considered to be in reserved occupations. So, for a short period, although I did not realise it, I was not employed. But, wait! It was not long before someone knew of my situation, as one morning I saw a stranger arrive at our yard. Little did I know, that this man was to be my next boss. After some consultation with Mrs Bowen, he approached me with the offer of a hiring for the next year. Due to this situation, Mr Bowen was to lose me even though I was not to join the RAF. When I explained this to Mr Bowen he said that if I had told him, that he would have kept me as well my replacement.

In the two years that I had been at the Moor, my sister Betty had got married and this year, my sister Mary had also married - 1938. Such was the situation in those days, that I had not attended Betty's wedding, this was not unusual, as it would mean a day off, and this was not 'on', although I did attend Mary's wedding. This was the end of my time at the Moor and when it came, once again I could not say that I was glad, but I could say that I had achieved another of my childhood ambitions - I had actually been able to replace, one of the grown-up workers at Moor. I went down the, now familiar, farm road, towards the main road, and as I went, I thought of the time that I had run this mile to catch a bus, which I could see on the top of the Cross Inn hills, it meant that I had to cover the one mile, while the bus travelled approximately two, with one stop to pick up waiting passengers. I thought also of the duel I had, when cycling the nine miles to Carmarthen to beat the bus. To pass it at each stop, and then be passed in between.

Whilst at the Moor I had achieved a lot of my ambitions but little did I know that my greatest ambition was yet to come, as the RAF was very much in my mind. The stranger that I had mentioned earlier, at the Moor, was a Mr Jones, better known as Johnny Jones of Great Newton farm near Llanddowror, this was the village that mother and father originated from. I had agreed to work for Mr Jones for the next year. I would be getting about £35 to £38 per annum. So it was that my 'box' was collected and I was to arrive later at Great Newton to start my new contract.

Newton, as it was usually referred to, was a big farm, three hundred acres, this was twice the size of the Moor and was the biggest farm in the area. It was situated on high ground and it offered a panoramic views of the surrounding countryside. One could see two other farms within view, Cwmbrwyn and Trecoed and I must not forget Penrallt where I was born.

The Jones family consisted of Mr Johnny Jones, Mrs Jones, two teenage daughters, Brenda and May and the youngest was a son of school age. He was named Ira, named, I believe after a famous wartime ace fighter pilot who was a close relative of the family. In addition to the family there was Eddie Phelps, Mrs Jones's brother and he was employed elsewhere. There was one more very important person, as far as I was concerned and that was Joe Johnson, Joey as he was called. He had worked there, in the same capacity as myself for two years and now we were to work together. There was one thing that was very evident from the beginning and that was the striking similarity between Joey and me. We were approximately the same age, same size, very similar features, especially the Welsh nose and it turned out that we were near identical in our work outlook and ability.

So, quite soon, life turned out to be one big competition. Joey had the advantage of being there for two years and was now, where I had yet to prove myself. Life here would be different, due to the fact that in other places I had worked alone . Where there would be more than one labourer on a farm, the work was divided between 'cows and horses' and you were either a cowman or a ploughman. Here, Joey was the cowman and I was at my favourite work with the horses. Apart from the specifics, the general work we would do together during the day and there was a lot of that. As we were workmates during the day, we also went out together in the evenings to various pubs etc. – usually on Joey's motor bike – (no breathalysers).

I have mentioned before, the practice of sleeping in or sleeping out, well, here we slept in and the house door was never locked. One advantage was that there was the opportunity of a bit of 'supper'. This would be left out on the table and two young lads, like Joey and I, really appreciated this, as we were usually hungry. This was not for the lack of food, as the food here was good and our quarters, bedroom, was comfy. This was situated on the third floor as it was a fairly big house. As a family, we all got on very well. There was one thing different from previous situations and that was that Mrs Jones was from Pembrokeshire and as this area was known as 'Little England beyond Wales' very little Welsh was spoken there. So, Mrs Jones, the two daughters and Eddie spoke English, while Mr Jones, Joey, Ira and I spoke Welsh. Strange, maybe, but I did not think much about it before. Although I did not realise it at the time, I had graduated from one farm size to another, till I had reached the top and I was now as high as I could go.

Up to now, I had been working on my own and although I had a good idea of my capacity for work before, I could now compare my standards with Joey, especially as we were so closely matched. So, it soon became evident that our efforts were to be very competitive. In the various jobs that we did together, it was accepted that we both did our best and it was more or less, always a race to try and beat each other.

In the first few winter months at Newton, Joey and I did a lot of work together and few people realised that when working in fields, you can see a long way, over a lot of country, but it means that a lot of people can see you and what you are doing. If for instance you would be muck-spreading, it was always set out in rows and we would do a row each, so it was not difficult to assess the progress. As I mentioned, we were fairly well matched, but I did remember on some occasions, when Joey was getting a little behind, he would revert to quality as opposed to quantity. I did not think that we were much different, on the other hand when I was talking to a neighbour, Willy Penrallt, he said to me 'It was about time somebody came to beat Joey', and inferred that I had done this, so it must have been noticed, but Joey and I were good pals and we got on well together.

Winter soon went into spring and on a farm this is the busy time, with all the preparation, the planting of corn and other crops and the treatment of the hay fields. I think it is interesting to mention here, that the pesticides and 'nasties' used today had not been heard of. We used all natural fertilisers, I think that I remember them all. There was 'basic slag' - sulphate of ammonia and super phosphate, and that was it. All this work was done by horses and it was hard work and very long hours. I had, Scott - Daisy - Diamond - Doxie - four big shire horses. These were in regular use, there were others out in the fields. These all had individual characters and I got to know them all well. The time had now come for me to do my ploughman's job. The ratio of land to be ploughed, was about one third, a hundred acres. So, I was to spend most my time out in the fields, just me and my horses and on nice sunny days this could be very pleasant. I would start early in the morning, come in for lunch, or dinner as we knew it, but as I worked up to six o'clock, my tea was usually brought out to the field, by one of the girls, or even Mrs Jones, a nice walk for them. I would sometimes use two horses as a team or depending on the job, I would have three, side by side. While ploughing, we would travel back and for across the fields so many times that the horse

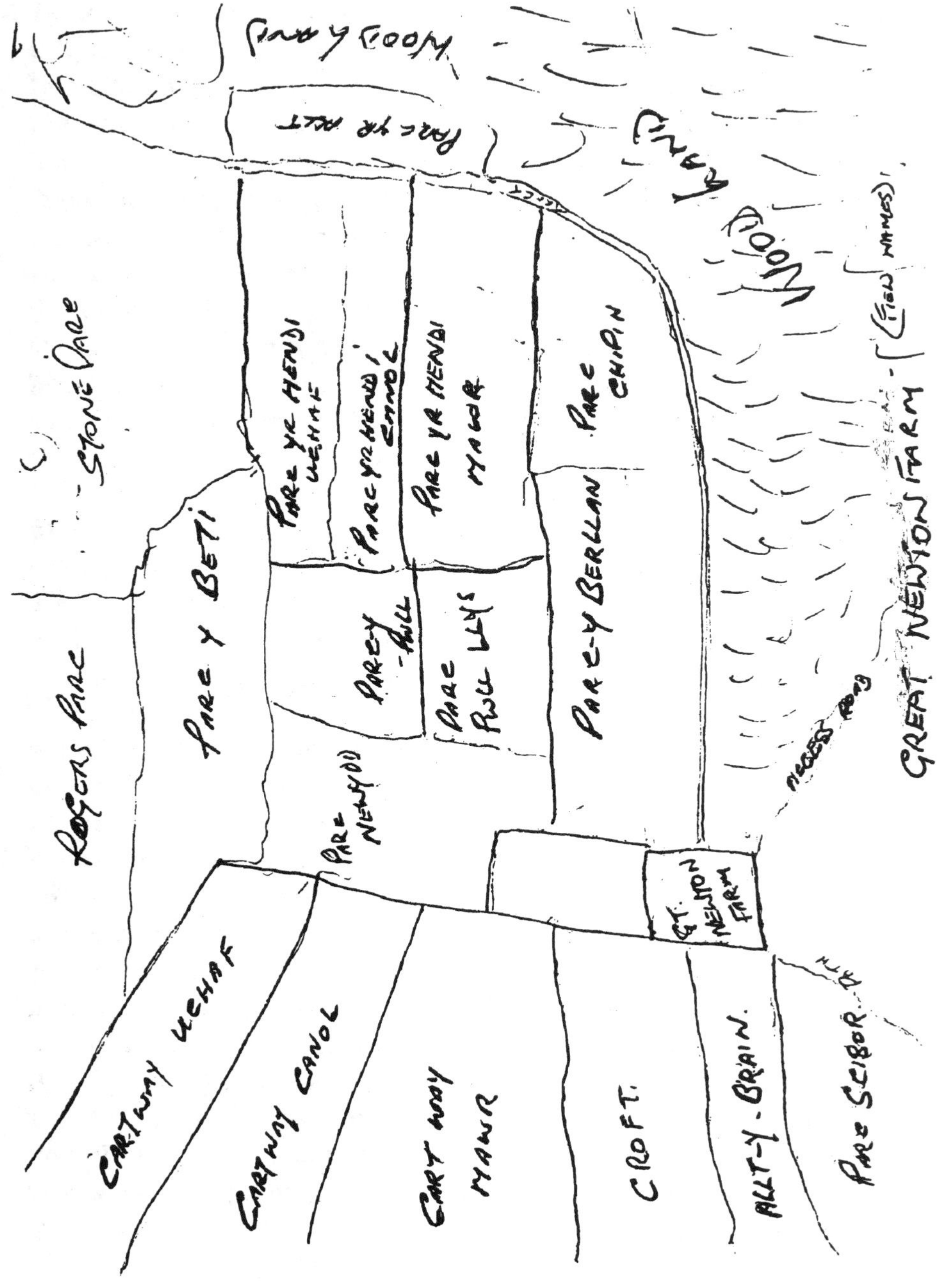
WOOD LAND
PARC YR ALLT
WOOD LAND
STONE PARC
ROGERS PARC
PARC Y BETI
PARC YR MENDI UCHAF
PARC YR MENDI CANOL
PARC YR MENDI MAWR
PARC CHIPIN
PARC-Y-BERLLAN
PARC-Y-PWLL
PARC PWLL LLYS
PARC NEWYDD
GT. NEWTON FARM
CARTWAY UCHAF
CARTWAY CANOL
CART WAY MAWR
CROFT.
ALLT-Y-BRAIN.
PARC SCIBOR
ACCESS ROAD
GREAT NEWTON FARM - (FIELD NAMES)

would get used to the repetition and would often only need a word or two from me.

Then would come the time when all the corn had been sown and all the root crops were in the ground, and while we had been doing this, the hay had been growing and now summer was with us and hay-making, once more and this as we now know, was a long hard working period for us and the horses. Very often in the summer you had to forget about the evening that you had planned to go out.

It was just 'hard luck'. When we did go we would really enjoy ourselves, it was like you work hard and you play hard'. We would often be very late coming in. I remember one evening, coming home after a few drinks, and hungry as usual. We came indoors to find the usual on the table, with a cloth covering it, but we were surprised to find a big rice "pud". We did not know whether it was meant for us or not, however, after we had devoured it, we then decided that it was more than likely for Sunday lunch, as this was Saturday night (too late!)

As I mentioned earlier, on a farm, the seasons determine the programme; the next phase would be the corn harvest. This follows on closely from the hay harvesting, but like all British summers, there are days when you have rain, so these would be days spent doing more menial jobs like cutting thistles in the grazing fields; Joey and I would work together on this with a scythe each.

It was now 1938/39 and to set the record straight, myxomatosis, the horrible disease to finish off the rabbits had not yet hit this country, so you can imagine a farm like Newton, with all the corn, grass and root crops, it was a paradise for rabbits. On many farms the task of trapping these was usually put out to contract, but not at Newton, as Mr Jones (boss) and Joey, did the trapping as well as everything else. I remember Joey 'whipping' round the traps early in the morning and coming back with a sack full of rabbits. The pony by the way was always in the stable, saddled up ready for use (a kind of taxi). I still had my little jaunts around the field in the evening with the gun, but I looked more for pigeons, it was more fun. It was customary on Christmas day and on New Years day to have a 'shoot'. We would go out, the boss, Joey, me and Ira, fairly early and return for dinner and we would sometimes go out again later. I remember a rather funny incident regarding Joey and his gun. It happened one day when we were working in the field, far away from the farmyard and as usual Joey and I were hungry, although we were really well fed, so Joey decided that he would go a short journey to Merry Moor. This was a smallholding owned by Mr Willy Davies, he was an egg merchant. He went in his van around the houses and farms, collecting eggs and at the same time carried items of groceries which he sold. Consequently his house was like a little shop, and the reason for Joey's visit was to buy some chocolate, at least this was what it started out as. After he had been away for some time, he came back carrying a double barrelled shotgun and he proceeded to tell me he had met the man from Merry Vale (not Merry Moor) - another place, and he had just shot two wild geese. He told Joey that the geese had landed in a field not far from where we were. So, off goes Joey to get a goose and sure enough, when he returned he was carrying a goose and that really could have been the end of the story. A few days later, when we were having dinner, another local farmer came to our door and asked for Joey - it appeared that he was rather annoyed with him, as he was, as he put it, three geese short in his flock. Yes the goose that Joey had shot and the other two were really tame domestic geese and he wanted compensation. He did not know at that time that his goose was being eaten for dinner. A fact which is not widely known, is that tame geese, during the leaner time of the year, when they are not fat, can and do, take off on occasional flights , this was one.

I have already covered the subject of hay harvesting and of course the main subject of my story 'The Horse' - there is however a further angle that has not been explained or highlighted and this is a very

HARVEST TIME

It is a warm summer's morn.
The sun is already high.
There's a little morning mist around
But not a cloud in the sky.

Where better than a farmyard
To greet such a lovely morn,
In the silence of the country
Among'st the hay and corn.

Summer time is harvest time,
Time to make the hay,
Time to gather in the crops
And store it all away.

From the haystack in the yard
Comes the smell of previous labours,
Hay that was carted yesterday
With the help of all our neighbours.

While out there in the field,
There's another crop to harvest.
When the morning dew has risen
We will have to work our hardest.

In the field the hay is collected
With a pitchfork and a rake,
Made into convenient 'tumps'
And left a while to 'make'.

Cont/

Now it's nearly time
To really make a start,
The neighbours are arriving,
One with a horse and cart.

We need a man to make the load,
Two to pitch the hay.
Someone has to lead the horse,
So for me – no school today.

We will move along from tump to tump,
Shout a warning as we go.
If I forgot to do so –
I would surely get to know.

There's a cask of beer for the thirsty.
Good food is being prepared.
Hot buns for our teas,
For supper – nothing spared.

When the day is over
And the sun disappears,
Men will still be working
'Till darkness interferes.

They will wake up in the morning
To yet another summer's morn,
To labour with other harvests,
Still gathering hay and corn

strange angle - from the horses point of view. I will explain this 'angle' later.

This all happened of course before the 'tractor era' and even before rubber tyres were used on carts and farm implements. Cart wheels were of wooden construction, with spokes and an iron band around the outside. In the hay harvest the horse was the main factor. It was involved in one way or another in all the job. The horse and cart was the only vehicle for carrying hay. Several differerent versions of the cart were used. The one used in harvesting was known as 'the Gambo'. It was constructed mostly of wood - it had a long 'body' indeed it was sometimes called the 'Longbody'. It was open at each end and the sides were slatted. For the purpose of haymaking poles were fitted to each corner, these would be about seven to eight feet long. This made an ideal vehicle for carting loads of hay, with an overall height of approximately twelve feet.

Loading or in other words, making a load of hay was rather a specialised job, it required a lot of practice. The object was really to carry as much as possible so the vehicle just mentioned was only a framework on which to build. As the load progressed beyond the outline and reached out in all directions including forward over the poor horse. A good load covered the horse leaving just the head and neck visible.

In those days the hay loader was just coming into use. This was attached to the cart and towed behind it was really a kind of elevator collecting the windrow of hay and carrying it upwards into the cart. This was of course an added strain for the horse so an extra horse was used in front of the shaft horse. All the horses were the biggest shire horses and could carry immense loads. This kind of handling of the hay has been replaced by the baler, and hay is thought of in bales and of course is a lot easier to handle. When it was handled loose a load could be twelve feet high and travelling to the hay barn in the farmyard could entail going through two or three fields with a gateway between each. It could also entail travelling along slopes. The horse was controlled by the man on top of that load, by means of a line. The 'drivers' view from the top of the load was a mass of hay with just the horses head and neck showing. Good loads were long and wide and this made it difficult getting through the gateways.

The purpose of writing this is to try and portray the problem from the poor horse's angle. I am now going to explain what happened when one of these loads tipped over as they sometime did - usually when negotiating a slope, laying the poor horse on it's side on the ground. It was fixed between the shafts still attached by chains and harness and through no fault of its own, found itself in this frightening situation. The natural inclination was to rise to the upright position but this is not possible but in its attempt it repeatedly beat its head in an up and down action, not forgetting that the horse is still on its side. So you can see that there is a serious risk of injury by the repeated connection with the ground. So it is the duty of the horseman to jump on and sit on the horse's head to hold it down until it can be freed from the harness and allowed to get up.

The autumn which was now approaching, was most probably the most important time/period of the year, as the crops, corn, oats, barley and root crops were food for the animals and the wheat which was sold for flour, were the result of our years work. The harvest had still to be gathered and so much depended on the weather. The progress and rate could only be according to horse power as the tractor had not yet appeared. The other factor was that, regardless of the weather, Sunday was a day of rest. The corn was cut by binder, drawn by three horses. The binder cut the corn, tied the sheaves and left them all in rows. These were collected by helpers and stood up in bundles of four to dry. After a considerable time in the field, the sheaves were carted to the rickland and made into ricks until later on when the threshing machine would come (remember in my early days when Ben drove the thresher).

THRASHING

A thrashing engine arrived today
To thrash the stack of corn.
It will be all set up and ready
To start tomorrow morn.

Early in the morning
When we've got up steam,
It will sound its hooter
To call the thrashing team.

Men will come from all around
In answer to its call,
Alloted to the various tasks,
Hard work for one and all.

The sheaves are fed into the drum
To whatever goes on inside it,
To emerge at the other end –
Agitated and divided!

The grain is carried to the loft
In many bulging sacks,
The straw, gathered by many hands
To form brand new stacks.

Cont/

When the thrashing is all over
And we've thrashed out all the grain,
The straw, neatly stacked away –
It will be time to move again.

Then down the lane we travel
Over many humps and bumps,
Dropping little bits of chaff
In occasional tell-tale lumps.

We will stop to pick up water
As it crosses o'er the stream,
Filling up its boiler,
Which it will then convert to steam.

Then with more steam and puffing,
It goes slowly on its way,
To arrive at another farmyard
For another thrashing day

I was to have two important jobs in the harvesting and threshing of the corn - jobs which I had not done before. As I was now in a senior position, the first job was to make the corn ricks, not an easy job. Corn in those days had many impurities in it, the worst being thistles. The sheaves are mostly handled with pitchforks, that is everywhere except when making the rick, when you have to use your hands and put your knee on each sheaf, to ensure that the sheaves are properly and securely placed in the shaping of the rick. The problem of the thistles is at its worst when the incoming loads are high and the rick maker is on the ground. The sheaves are thrown down and sometimes around your ears, not pleasant, especially as the thistles are now drying out to a crisp brown condition.

During the season I was also involved in helping other farmers in the harvest, this was the only way that the labour required became available - by helping each other. This was very necessary when the thresher came to thresh out the corn. Each and everyone had their own individual job dealing with the sacks of corn and straw, but usually I was the man that fed the sheaves of corn into the drum of the thresher, not the heaviest job but a responsible one.

There were, if you remember, two other fairly big farms, Cwmbrwyn and Trecoed, not far away - incidentally my father had worked at both of these places before my time. I did hear it said, that Mr Jones (boss), Mr Evans Trecoed, and Mr Bowen Cwmbrwyn, would meet on Sunday evening in a little cottage called the Grammer. Now, two of these at least were pipe smokers and Tilly the lady, that lived in Grammer, said that between them they nearly put her fire out, with their spitting.

I was now twenty years old and I had not started smoking but around this time I started to have the occasional cigarette when I was out in the pubs and it was not much later that it became a regular habit. I then started smoking a pipe during the day, I suppose I wanted to feel 'grown up'. Incidentally there was no talk of cigarettes causing cancer in those days. It was just the cost that limited the amount - six old pence per packet of ten. That was just over two and half new pence. To start with it was great fun to go around the fields puffing at that pipe. I remember one day, I only had one match, so I decided that if I kept stoking tobacco on top of the old, I could keep it going - great fun! I also remember when walking to St Clears, one night, a distance of some five or six miles, I would light my pipe when I started and I would try to keep it going as long as possible to see how many miles I could do with a pipeful.

We did walk a lot during our nights out as we did have some! I do remember what we used to get up to on our way home - like, one night going into a cornfield which had been cut - the sheaves were in stooks (four sheaves leaning against each other). We thought that we would rearrange them. We collected as many as we could and made a huge stack. Imagine the farmer's surprise when he saw that - harmless I suppose, when compared with today's pranks.

I had now nearly completed my year at Newton and we were in the autumn. A time when all the harvest had been gathered, and we would soon be back to the time when I first arrived, but now we would be catching up after the busy time. In those days lime was used on grassland, the lime was delivered in its raw form - limestones. This was placed in long heaps in the corner of the field, covered with soil and left for a few weeks. The result of this exercise would be that the stones would have all powdered and would mix with the soil, this then would be carted out and spread on the grassland. One morning, Joey and I embarked on the lime carting exercise with a horse and cart each. We had filled and carted several loads and my cart was about half full again, Joey noticed something amongst the cows, grazing nearby. One of the cows had been let out after milking, with a rope tied tightly around its belly - it was common practice when a cow kicked during milking, but of course it should have been taken off before the cow was let out. The rope was usually tied in a loop, with a piece dangling, so Joey and I, being the energetic type, thought that if we went quietly up to the cow, one on each side, one of us could grab the end, pull it, and hope that it would release the rope. 'Good idea'. When we tried it out, the cow had other ideas, it made a dash and frightened the rest of the herd and the whole lot stampeded. As if this was not bad enough, I looked around to where the horses and carts were and I saw my horse and cart disappearing in a cloud of lime dust, the faster the horse ran, the more dust. The commotion had frightened the horse. I now had to do something but I was not dressed in running gear as I had a canvass sack tied around me.. However, no time to consider dress, I decided to make for the other side of the field and as the horse was going around the field while I crossed it, I met it on the other side and so I stopped another runaway. We eventually finished the carting and covered the whole field in heaps, ten yards apart. A few days later it was our lot to spread these lime heaps. We started early one morning and planned to do as much as possible and by working in echelon we avoided each other's dust. We completed the whole ten acres in one day. So when the boss told us to continue the next day, he could not believe us when we said that we had finished - another record I am sure.

The time was now approaching the end of the hired year, so, around October, it was time to consider whether I was going to stay or indeed whether the boss wanted me to stay. The feeling was mutual and it was agreed that I stay for another year and I am glad to say that the same applied to Joey, so we had another year together.

Newton was a mixed farm, with three hundred acres of land. One hundred was arable, the rest supported the various animals. There were store cattle that wintered out, some two hundred sheep, and young unbroken horses, one and two year olds. There was of course the herd of about thirty milk cows. As the young horses became old enough, I was involved in breaking them in. Some of course were sold at the horse fairs that I mentioned earlier. I remember on one occasion, a young two year old that I was breaking, I decided one Sunday morning to take it for an outing to the field. I had a problem with this one in so far as, while I could lead it anywhere, but when I went behind it, it turned around to face me. To try and overcome this problem, I decided to drive it up alongside a hedge, and if I prevented it turning one way, the hedge would prevent it from going the other way. I remember it was a damp morning and the grass was wet. The next thing that happened was that my horse jumped over the hedge and I had to go with it (we got over the hedge, but not the problem). We eventually put the horse in shafts, so that it could not turn.

The boss took the milk to the St Clears factory every morning in the van and when he returned, he would take the pony, that was already saddled and with his faithful dog, would do his round of the stock. The winter came and went and before you knew it you were on the second round of the routine. I still had the same horses which I worked and looked after. They were well fed, like all my animals. Food was plentiful, as the loft above the stable was full of corn. When the boss had the occasion to use any of the horses, he would remark that I fed them too well and they were frisky. I got to know my horses for their individual characters. Scott, a full-sized shire, was big slow and very strong. Doxie, the youngest, and still developing, very friendly, she had a habit of turning round and biting me when I groomed her, ticklish, I suppose. Daisy, the one that made the lime run, but Diamond was the one that needed special treatment, she was extremely nervous. When I worked them I could have any combination of the four. I remember an incident when I was helping with the haymaking at The Mill (Patties) the hayfield was rather boggy and I remember in those days we had not the rubber tyre era. Usually on these occasions I would be working with horse and cart making the load and as the ground was soft, a second horse was put in front of the shaft horse, attached by two long chains. It happened that Diamond was the extra front horse and someone else was driving her. They got bogged down with the load and could not get out. I saw the problem and went to help. To get out of the situation, you had to get both horses to pull at the same time and the best way to achieve this was to give your command urgently, and loudly. This frightened poor Diamond so much, that I saw the links in the chain flatten with the strain, but it did the trick and we were free

My second year had started, very much the same. I worked the horses, doing the ploughing etc., but something was to change all this, I suppose you could call it progress. The boss bought a tractor, a new innovation in those days. I remember it arriving, it was the most popular model of that time, a Fordson. Now, I must have seen this as a threat to my job, as it was meant to replace the horses. Who was going to drive it? It did not seem that anyone knew, as it was put in a shed, the doors closed and nothing was said about it for a while. This was progress and you cannot stop it I suppose. Gradually the tractor was taken out and driven around and one day when I was ploughing with my team, lo and behold, this thing appeared in the field and it had a brand new plough behind it. The boss and Joey had decided to try it out. I did not like this situation, I was the ploughman, was I going to drive it? Did I really want to ? Was this a threat to my favourite job? Well as it happened, it was progress and the mechanisation of the job was soon to prove very effective. It was not a complete change, as the horses were to be used for yet a while. I somehow gradually got used to the idea and did a lot of work with the tractor. I had for some time been thinking of the RAF but my work with horses was a satisfying job and I had a kind of tug-of-war, trying to decide which I really wanted and this latest episode made me think once more of joining the RAF if I was allowed to.

Joey and I still got on very well together and we would go out together especially at weekends. There was a funny incident that happened one Saturday night. If you remember, we were always thinking of eating, even though we were well fed. We decided that this Saturday night, we would collect some eggs from the chicken's nests and hide them so that we could boil them when we arrived home late.

We came home and as the fire was always 'going' it was not long before we had the saucepan with half a dozen eggs in, on the fire. There was one thing that we had overlooked. We heard a motor bike arriving, and we knew that Eddy Phelps - Mrs Jones's brother, would be in in a few moments, so action, Joey grabbed the boiling saucepan with the eggs and put it in the settle -this was a wooden seat with a back and the seat was a lid that opened up. He popped the lot in there and we waited. Eddy arrived and sat on the settle, just above the eggs. We thought that we were clever, until the steam started to come out around Eddy. As he had 'had a few' he did not seem to notice, he soon went to bed and we had our eggs.

Although I did not know it at the time, there were other changes to come during the second year. First of all, Mr Bowen, Cwmbrwyn, died. He was, remember, one of the three farmers mentioned earlier. He was a bachelor, so he employed a maid, come housekeeper, called Muriel, that Joey had been going out with for some time. As time passed, I saw less and less of him in the evenings, due to his courting.

I still enjoyed a certain amount of my horse work in the fields, and as the ploughman, avoided or should I say did not get involved in, the milking and the other routine around the farmyard. I would stay out in the fields until quite late and in the autumn I have memories of coming home down the lane, after a long warm day, along the edge of the woods, where the owls hooted. Owls were numerous, I suppose that they were barn owls. They sheltered in the various farm buildings, especially the hay barns. I would often find their droppings. These were the occasions when I would wonder whether this life was better than the RAF. This was never very far from my mind. During the latter part of my second year at Newton Mr Evans, Trecoed, passed away, this meant that Mr Jones, my boss, was the only one left of the three. During my time at Newton, although I cannot remember exactly when, my mother and father moved, yet again -from Cwrt-y-Bedw to Bronyglyn, a smaller place near Bancyfelin, not too far away. It was unfortunate that the owner of Cwrt-y-Bedw wanted to sell the place. The daughter of another farm nearby and her husband, wanted to buy it. There was something not strictly straight about the deal - it seemed rather underhanded. I was sad really as I had some pleasant memories of Cwrt-y-Bedw. I did visit the place several times in later years and I was very suprised to find, on one of my visits, the burned out shell of the house. The place was derelict.

Joey and I continued to work together a good deal of the time but these days were numbered as he was soon to marry his girlfriend, Muriel, from Cwmbrwyn. In the meantime we continued to have our little bit of fun. This occasion involved the fruit man. He was one of those people who travelled around farms and cottages selling the few items that he carried in a bag - remember I mentioned these kind of people when I was in Broad Moor. He would have cheap items and in addition, he would have fruit, cigarettes, matches, sweets and chocolate. He would usually arrive at mid-afternoon on Thursday. Well this Thursday, we were, yes believe it or not, hungry and looked forward to a few bars of chocolate. As we were a little way from the farmyard, Joey volunteered to go and look to see if he was around. I waited in anticipation for his return. Well, I did not have long to wait. I saw Joey coming, with the goods in a paper carrier bag. Joey had a smile on his face, when he shared out the contents. He gave me two stones and kept two stones! Joey's joke - we had missed the fruit man. As it happened this turned out to be Joey's last joke, as soon after this he got married and left. He eventually had a farm of his own and although I did not see him again, I know that he retired when he was about fifty.

Life was never to be the same again, without Joey, as we had got to be good working pals. After about three months, Joey's replacement arrived. He was Vincent James a married man, the son of Mrs Sophia James, the Mwntan, a small farm not far away. She was the midwife that delivered me into this world 'small world'. However, Vincent was married, and was to live in the cottage called Little Newton. This was the situation, as I started yet another year, my third at Newton. I had agreed a salary for next year of fifty two pounds. So far as the RAF was concerned, I had to 'soldier on' as the saying goes, only in reserve. I was still in a reserved occupation.

Life was indeed very different with Vincent. Although he was a Welsh man he did not speak Welsh. This alone was a barrier. The atmosphere that had existed between Joey and myself was no longer there - gone was the competitive spirit, I found it rather unreal, but maybe this was the real, if so then Joey and I had been different. I tried to still carry on the normal routine, such as getting up as we had always done, sometimes earlier than others, this was always earlier than the boss, but with Vincent living in his cottage, we were often at different programmes. For a while this went on in a kind of a new routine, but unfortunately, this showed Vincent in an inferior light. I did not even realise the situation was developing as a result of this, but the boss must have appreciated it.

My evening outs had also been affected since Joey left, I now had to revert back to my cycling habit, as I still had my bike. I got to know another farm labourer, who worked in Glandwr farm, at the bottom of our road, he was called Tom. We used to visit the 'local' in Llanddowror in the evening and walk back the short-cut, through the fields. I remember one morning, finding that I had several thorns in my hands, we had apparently fallen together, into some brambles, on our way home the previous night.

After a few more months, I was offered a motor-bike, if I wanted to buy it. I remember it was a Triumph 350cc, but it had a slight defect, as the second gear was not working. The other problem was, of course, that I did not have a driving licence. However, I bought it for seven pounds, not much you may say, but it was seven weeks wages. This was something new to me so, I had to learn to master it and although

I say it myself, I got quite good at it, in spite of the absence of second gear. Now, you may wonder, what on earth would I do with a motor bike that I was not licensed to ride, but, somehow I ended up using it to travel the distance of approximately three miles, over the quiet country roads, to the main road, where I would then catch a bus into town and then the ride the motor-bike home again later. Sometimes I had a drink or two, which made the tale that I will now tell, a little funnier. For reasons that I do not necessarily have to mention (not important really) but I could not start the bike in the normal way by kick-starting it, so, I had to resort to running down a hill, and starting it that way. That posed no problem, as in Wales there a plenty of hills - but, I experienced my difficulty. As I approached the top of a big hill, about three quarters of the way up, my engine cut out. Now, as the only means of starting again was to run down the hill - remember? Down I go and 'brum' it starts, now turn around, problem solved, but no, at the very same spot it stops again. So, down we go to start, and it appears up we went to stop. As it happened, each time at the same spot. Eventually I ended up pushing the bike up the last bit and of course it was then downhill the other side. I later discovered the reason for this strange behaviour, the petrol pipe was partially blocked with a bit of fluff (not the kind that you carried on the Pillion) and it meant that when it required that extra bit of petrol, it was not available.

The next episode is rather a sad one, it concerns Vincent, who had been at Newton about four or five months. For some reason, completely unknown to me at the time, the boss asked me if I would be prepared to carry on, on my own, if he gave Vincent the sack. At that time, I really did not think that it was anything that I had done, but now, with hindsight, I think it must have been due to my own performance (work capacity); I said I would. However, it happened one morning very early, Vincent must have been later arriving that morning than usual. The boss met him and it appears, told him that he was finished. I do not know about the rights and wrongs of it, regarding notice etc. I did not hear any of the conversation, but Mrs

Jones told me later, that Vincent had said that he was not prepared to follow Wyndham. The boss apparently told Vincent that Wyndham had his reputation before he came to Newton. So that was the end of Vincent's job. I now wonder, what could I have done differently.

I was now on my own for the time being, cowman, plough man etc. Life did not change a lot. I suppose that with one man less, there would be less done. I would carry on my regular jobs, but now I was called upon to help with the cattle. I had of course, been a cowman and ploughman combined, when I worked on previous farms. At Newton there was a herd of what was known as beef cattle or store cattle. Some of these were born out as calves and had never been anywhere other than the fields, which they roamed freely, unlike the dairy herd, which was housed in winter and were well fed. The store cattle were mainly young steers or bullocks, most about two years old, and at the end of the second summer, they would be big, fat, fit and wild. This is the time that they would be sold for beef. Now, you will remember, when I was at school I mentioned Tom Bevan, the cattle drover, he would go round collecting cattle, bought by the dealers and would take them to the rail head for transportation. Well this system had now died out. Maybe the old drovers had gone and had not been replaced and we had not yet reached the trucking system, that came later. So it was that in this 'climate' that I got involved in 'driving' some of these mavericks to market in St Clears.

St Clears store cattle market, was held each Thursday and as it had been decided to walk four bullocks to market, I started fairly early in the day, so as to arrive at the market in good time. I was to go alone, driving from behind, maybe I was not entirely alone, as I had 'Cora', one of the best sheep dogs that you could wish for. As we started out along the quiet country road, Cora would travel most of the way, in the field, on the other side of the hedge, adjacent to the road, and if there was a gap anywhere, she would be there waiting, to prevent the cattle going through as we passed, she would be off to the next gap.

So, we all went along the country road quite well and I had no idea of the drama to come. It happened when we reached the streets, over the bridge. The cattle had been getting more and more unsettled, the farther we got from home and now among the houses, shops etc, they must have felt hemmed in. I distinctly remember how it started; there was one steer to be the leader. For the purpose of this story we can call him Charlie. As he walked up close to the shop windows, he saw his reflection in the windows and I thought for a moment that he was going to attack it and this was his first attempt to go back home, the first of many. We managed however, to get a little further along up to side road entrance by Harry Griffiths's shop. This was less than halfway through the village, anyway Charlie decided that this could be a way of getting back home. It was in fact a loop road that joined the main road, about four hundred yards further back. Now, it was apparent that I had problems and by now I had a few helpers. Some of the helpers looked after the other three bullocks, while I chased after Charlie. Everything had now increased in speed, as it seemed that this beast was determined to go home, or at least away from these strange surroundings. One would be surprised how fast a beast like that can run and it seemed that he was beyond the control of the dog. I chased it out to the main road and up to where we had left the others, only to find, that in spite of whatever we did, Charlie went exactly the same way, in by Harry Griffiths and out to the main road again. I now found that I was getting more and more people trying to help, but this did not deter Charlie. This 'vicious circle' was to occur a total of seven times, after which, Charlie became even more determined. On his way round the circle, he took another turn which brought us out by the bridge and nearer home; so it seemed at last that he had won, but not yet, I was after him as fast as I could go, I even managed to get up alongside and with my stick I hit out at his eyes and I was fortunate enough to stop him and turn him around and with the help of some more people, we managed to keep Charlie on the main road, join up with the others three and with many helpers, we did pass the farthest point and we even got past Harry Griffiths's shop. We were once more altogether, dog and all, but we still had a good half mile of the village to get through to the mart. We got as far as the Blue Boar crossroads, before Charlie decided that there was still hope. We had just passed the County Council depot and it was here that Eddie Phelps, (Mrs Jones, Newtons brother) worked. The news of our journey had reached them ahead, so they were all outside when we went past. When Charlie made his next attempt, a few minutes later, they were all across the road, with shovels etc and this did stop Charlie.

So away we went once more, now nearly in sight of the cattle market, where Mr Jones, my boss, would be waiting and I had got the cattle within a hundred yards of our destination, when one of the other steers decided to go off the road, around the Gwalia Hall building. I go round to drive it out, this I did and arrived once I more on the road, only to find Charlie disappearing down the road towards home. So, here I go up once more to the council depot and believe it or not, the men were once more across the road, but this time Charlie did not stop, we both went flying through the line of men, I now had to do something. I was running alongside Charlie and I did the same as I had done before, I hit him on his eye and once more we turned around. This was Charlie's last attempt, as we eventually reached the mart very much later than was intended, all present and correct. After the cattle were penned in the boss took me into a nearby pub and I had the choice of whatever I wanted to drink with no limits.

This then had been the most difficult task that I had ever carried out. It had all started out just as a cattle drive, but when I left Charlie in that iron pen, I was sorry for him and somehow wished that with such determination that we both could have won.

To assist in understanding this epic event I have drawn up a brief sketch of our route.

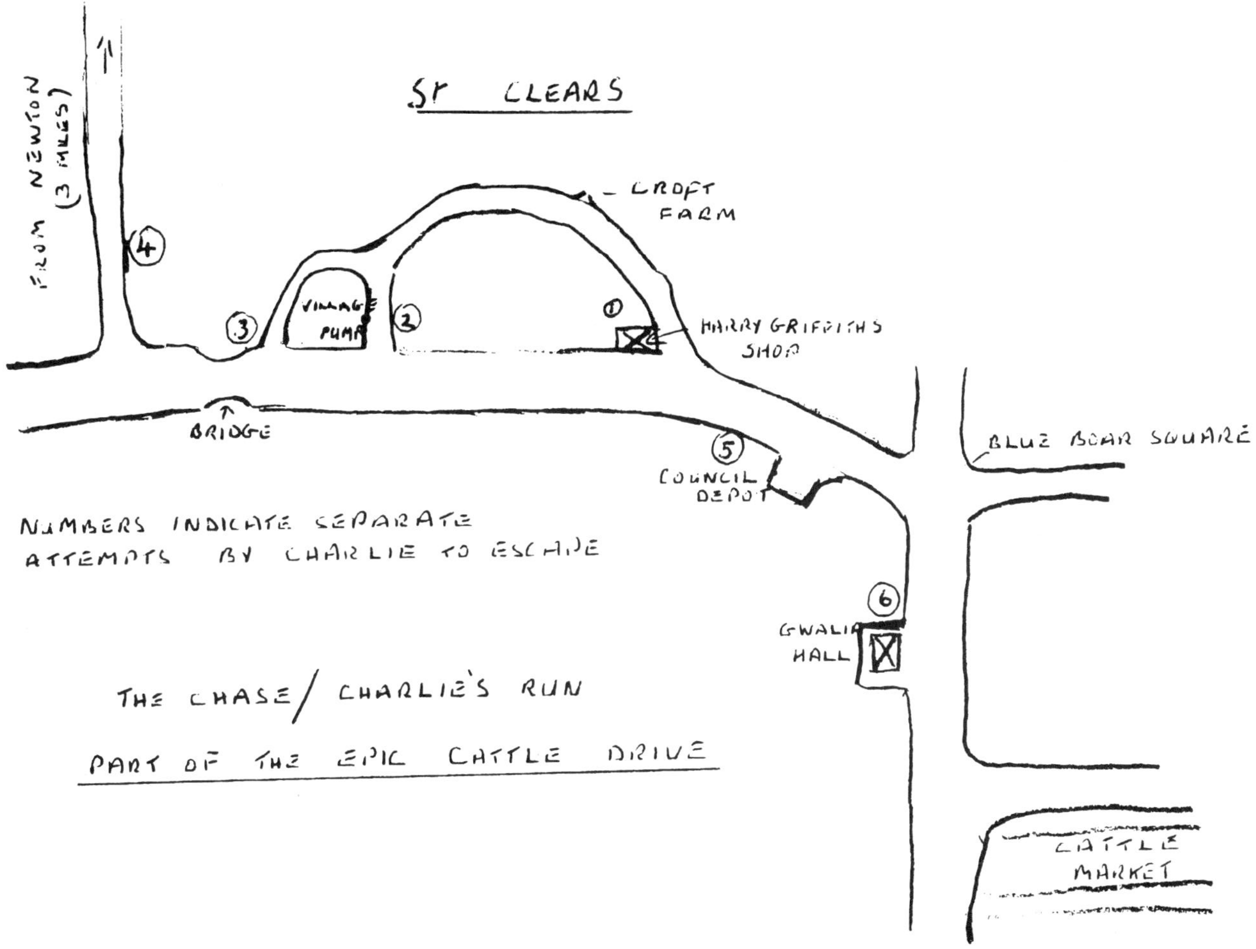
ST CLEARS
FROM NEWTON (3 MILES)
CROFT FARM
VILLAGE PUMP
HARRY GRIFFITHS SHOP
BRIDGE
COUNCIL DEPOT
BLUE BOAR SQUARE
GWALIA HALL
CATTLE MARKET
NUMBERS INDICATE SEPARATE ATTEMPTS BY CHARLIE TO ESCAPE
THE CHASE/ CHARLIE'S RUN
PART OF THE EPIC CATTLE DRIVE

After this life seemed to get back to normal, thank goodness, as we could not keep that kind of performance up for long. I seem to remember about this time, we had a little 'addition' to the staff in the form of a little boy called Olly. He was just fourteen years old as this was the school leaving age in those days. This of course was the age that I started but I did not think then that it was very young (strange). I was still no nearer joining the RAF but I had applied and received some literature which I found very interesting. This had been quite an eventful period, certainly a lot different to my first two years. We were once more in the midst of harvesting and all the other hard work, like singling and hoeing turnips etc., all done by hand.

By virtue of the time that I had been at Newton, living with the family every day, what happened next was a great shock to me, but not as much as it was to the family. The day started off in very much the same way as usual. I was in the kitchen when the boss came down, come to think of it, a little earlier than usual. He came just as I was about to leave, but I had mislaid my cap. He asked me what it was that I was looking for, I told him. He found and handed it to me and I went out. I had since Joey left, got more involved with the milking, as there were several cow-sheds close together. We all started in different sheds, that meant, Brenda, May, myself and the boss. It was about half an hour after we started, that Eddie Phelps came to me and asked me where the boss was. I assumed that he was in one of the other sheds, but Eddie was soon back and seemed in a very distressed state, to say that he had found the boss but he was dead. Eddie apparently discovered the body outside in the vicinity of the house. I could hardly believe that such an awful thing had happened. I thought that I was probably the last person that he had spoken to and at that time he seemed to be normal. One can but imagine the effect that this had on the family.

The next question, what would happen now? That is after the immediate arrangements for the funeral etc. Joey came to the funeral and we both carried the coffin. He was buried in the churchyard at Llanddowror. When this terrible thing happened, I had no idea that the boss had any problems, as everything on the farm was going well. Thinking back to the previous day though, and in particular to the previous evening, we, that is, boss, Olly and I, were working together in the potato field, and it would be difficult to say that the boss was quiet, as he was normally so. (He would sometimes just grunt in reply to your question). No, it was the fact that he was the boss, or gaffer, as Joey called him. He did not seem to be aware of the time, that is for finishing or going down to tea. I remember that I had to remind him (very unusual).

I have mentioned before that 'life would never be the same' well it never is, is it? This time it was certainly true. It seemed that we were on a ship, who's captain had died. But, life must go on, regardless, so I suppose that I carried on doing the things that I would have done anyway. I would, from a point of respect, confer with Mrs Jones, but it did not seem to be the same, as I did not think that I was doing it for anyone. This I suppose was due to my subservient nature, a quality, if you can call it that, that I have carried with me all through my life.

Eddie Phelps, who lived with us at Newton, worked for the County Council and had no connection with the work on the farm, but Mrs Jones had another brother Bob, from Pembrokeshire. He was a tractor plough man by trade and now he had come to help out at Newton. This I did not think was a good thing for me, as he was encroaching on my territory, the ploughing and the tractor work, which was my domain. This was, if you remember, the only job that I considered as may be equivalent to my ambition to join the RAF. So, now, as this was in doubt my thoughts turned once more to the RAF, this was of course, if I was allowed to join.

Now, Mrs Jones would very soon have to decide on the future of the farm, as the children had to be considered. Ira, here son, was about fourteen, a little young maybe. Anyway, he had already made his preference known by taking a job in a garage in Carmarthen. He was of course, too young for the services. Now, Brenda and May, like Ira had been born and grew up at Newton. I think that Brenda at least, would have liked to do something other than farming. These were some of the considerations that faced Mrs Jones. When it came to deciding, I was very surprised to find that I was a governing factor. Mrs Jones asked me if I would be prepared to stay, and if I did, she would keep on farming at Newton. Now, with hindsight, I think that this could have been an opportunity for a career in farming for me. I did not take up the offer. Somehow I did not think that life and work would be the same, especially if Bob stayed. They had thought of this, and Bob assured me that if I stayed he would not be involved in my ploughing job. I had already made up my mind to try the RAF again. So, eventually, Mrs Jones decided to sell Great Newton and consequently have a sale of all stock. Having made this decision, I now had to have some plans of my own.

The ultimate was always the RAF - would I be allowed to go? I had already had a few confrontations with the County War Agricultural Committee (C.W.A.C.) in Carmarthen. I think that there was some connection between the RAF and the C.W.A.C. or maybe the recruiting office. The reason for this assumption was that, each time I made an approach to the recruiting office, the man from the C.W.A.C. knew of it.

Time went by, and the sale passed, but by now the person who bought Newton, a Mr David, had naturally bought a lot of things at the sale and I had some involvement with him. In the interim period, I was assured by the C.W.A.C. that I was not allowed to volunteer for the RAF because I was in a reserved occupation, so, although I left Newton for a short period, Mr David enticed me back, he said, 'If only for a short period, to help me get started'.
Now, Newton with the Davids' was very different. Mr David, was by

background, a manager in a milk factory. His wife was a very nice person but as I was to find out, not very organised. They had three small children, Erith, aged seven, Gary, maybe four and a baby about one year old – so much for the family. Mr David had plans for the farm staff, this comprised of three worker - Emlyn, who was cowman, John, who was a shepherd and me, once more the horseman, ploughman. So it was in this new environment that I started again, or should I say, it was the beginning of the end of my farming career.

As far as I was concerned, I was just working here for a short period of time, before joining up, so I carried on my work, as I had done previously, but, it soon became evident that things were not working out. It seemed that the Davids were not very concerned with 'time', getting up, starting work, meal times, were just allowed to happen and the day was just as long as daylight.

Although I had tried hard to make things happen, things did not. A typical incident; in the morning, to allow me to go to the field to plough, it was agreed that I go before breakfast and that it would be brought out to me. However, it would be about eleven o'clock before Mrs David brought it (bless her). So, to try and keep things in order, or maybe, get things into order, I would still stop and go down for my lunch (dinner) at twelve o'clock, but of course this did not work, as there would not be any ready. Mr David had good intentions, but I am afraid that these never did materialise. He unfortunately suffered from drowsiness and often dropped off to sleep. He would take the milk to the factory in his van and as Newton was approached by a lengthy farm lane, mostly up hill, with a gateway halfway, which he would have to stop to open each time; at this point, he would often fall asleep in the driver's seat. Mrs David was aware of this and she would sometimes ask me to go and look for the boss and sure enough that was where I would find him.

The war had been going for some time and farmers were encouraged to grow more food for which they would receive subsidies. This encouraged them to plough more land, we already ploughed about 120 acres, which was a large chunk of the farm. Mr David was quite keen to cultivate the land and I was fully engaged in this. He mentioned to me one day that it would be a good idea to have shift work through the night. When I asked him how he intended to do this, he said that I would do the day work and he would do the night work. I could not see this happening although I did not say so, he could hardly keep awake during the day leave alone at night. Needless to say, it never happened.

I kept on getting various information from the RAF recruiting office and I realised that while I had been told I could not join up, I found out that if I volunteered for aircrew, the authorities could not stop me. So, it was along these lines that I managed to get some success. In December 1941, I was instructed to report to the recruiting office in Cardiff; so at last, I thought I was on my way. It was fortunate that my uncle Bill, my mother's brother lived in Cardiff. He was a retired railway inspector. Very stern and proper, with twisted ends to his moustache. However, I was pleased that I was to spend one night in his house, after he had accompanied me to the RAF recruiting office. The next morning I was to report to Penarth for attestation. For the first time in my life, I woke up that morning, in a town and when I looked out of the window, I saw Barrage balloons. When I got up, uncle Bill had already cooked me ham and eggs for by breakfast. I was then to catch a train to Penarth to be tested and return home. Uncle Bill asked me to call with him on my return as he had something he wanted me to take to my mum. Now, I travelled on the train with several other lads on the same mission as myself and when I returned, I was reluctant to lose contact with the lads, so I kept on the train and did not call with uncle Bill - black mark! He was not pleased, as I heard later. I had been tested for a trade and I was now awaiting a result. I was to learn later that I had passed the medical but had failed my written test. Not surprising really, as I was really out of my depth. I was informed that I had been assessed as a balloon operator, so it had worked; I was in on the ground floor but as I was in a reserved occupation, my call-up would be deferred to a later date, but 1 was in'. Meanwhile back in Carmarthen, somehow or other, the man from the County War Agricultural Committee heard of my success and he was 'on the war path'. I was instructed to come to Carmarthen to his office, and he drove me to his superior's office on the Esplanade, where they tried to get me to change my mind about the RAF. But, my mind had been made up for years and I was not likely to change it now. They then told me that if I continued with my plan, I would have to come back anyway. Well, I never did, not for a long time.

Meanwhile, back at the farm, I was as happy as a sand boy. I had the best of both worlds my super farm job and I was to be a member of the RAF. Life at Newton went on very much the same, although things were not perfect, we did some good work. Since my change to the Davids', I have not mentioned any special incidents. Maybe, it was one big incident! I suppose I could relate the case of the horse at Llanddowror. It happened when Mr David told me that he had bought a horse and that he would take me to collect it. I went to the field and caught the horse and prepared to ride it back to Newton. It was the hunter type; I mounted it and started to gallop to the other end of the field, but came to a big ditch across the middle; I pulled the horse up to stop it but it continued, so I tried harder, so hard that it reared up on its hind legs. I fell off backwards into the ditch and the horse came in on its back along with me. Later, back at Newton, when I was riding across a field, it did not stop when we approached a hedge, it took off and over we went. It was only after this incident that I was to learn, that what I had in this horse, was an ex-steeple chaser - surprise, surprise.

I did mention earlier that Mrs David was rather disorganised, well, I could mention a rather embarrassing incident. One of her problems, was that when Mr David went to town, she never knew, no one knew I suppose when he would return and he would often be bringing groceries that were required. On this particular day, late in the afternoon, she was waiting for his return, as it was past the time when we would be having our tea. All three of us were working close to the house, conveniently, I suppose. When Mrs David asked me to come in for tea, as you would expect, the other two started to come. 'No, only Wyndham' she said 'as I have only enough bread for one'. I had one very good friend amongst the David family and that was little Gary. He was possibly five by now, and he was very attached to me. He wanted to follow me around. I remember the day when he really wanted to come out into the field with me, but it would not have been very practical. His mum said that he cried for a long time after I left. Although he would not know of my service intentions, he would when he was annoyed with you say 'go and join the army' - little did he know. I was now on borrowed time, waiting for that day, when the postman would bring that all - important letter, but I was to spend another six months at Newton as my day for actually joining up, did not come until June 25th 1942. During this six months, things went along normally as I do not remember any more events. I worked just as hard as ever and although I was getting more than the agreed average wage for agricultural workers Mr David tried to entice me to stay. He said 'if money can keep you, you can stay', and he even made me an offer of a smallholding, with additional land, so that I could start farming on my own. Even this could not change my priority for the RAF, although, with hindsight, this was a marvellous opportunity, if I had the same choice again, I would choose as I did.

I realised that this was the end of my farming career for the time being, but when you are that age, the world is your oyster and nothing seems final. It was in one way the end of an era, but what was more important to me, it was the beginning of another adventurous journey.

SECTION II

CHAPTER IV

1942 ENLISTMENT IN THE RAF

I had been accepted and had been a member of the RAF since my attestation, six months earlier. I was classed as an Airman 2nd class with a number 1651975. Now the time came for me to actually join up and leave home for destinations unknown. The date I could never forget, neither did mother. Years later I discovered a little page from a note book, in a drawer and on it inscribed - Wyndham left for the forces June 25th 1942.

The morning of June 25th was as mother described it 'as if I was getting married' - with my ironed shirt cuffs and cuff links, white shirt of course! My first destination was once more Penarth, which was the recruiting place really, but we would be posted elsewhere for our (square bashing) which we later discovered was Blackpool. All activities in the RAF were very exciting for me, as first of all it was the company of other men I suppose, as opposed to working alone in the fields. The journey from Penarth to Blackpool was on a 'troop train'; a special train to take recruits. We were packed in, as many as possible to a compartment; a seat for each I suppose, but what about the 'kit'? This would take up as much room as the men. Kit bags and packs were pushed into all convenient places, especially on the racks above the seats. Now, the journey took many hours and troops were usually moved at night, when normal travel was at its lowest point. So we all settled down as 'comfy' as possible, many lying on the seat and on the floor. I remember waking up to find or feel something dripping on me from above. It turned out to be 'Silvo' a metal polish, from a can in someone's kit bag. This of course was used for cleaning the brass buttons etc. The someone had not put the cap on tight. The liquid polish had dripped on my new uniform and proved very difficult to remove. 'Happy days' or was it nights!

We were an entry and as such we were kept together for the first period of training - 12 weeks 'square bashing' as it was commonly known, so called I suppose because of the time spent on the drill square - the drilling, that was yet to come. When we eventually arrived at Blackpool Central Station, we disembarked and were formed into squads, to be marched off to the various hotels and guest houses which had all been taken over by the 'War Office', mainly for the RAF. I was to be accommodated in a guest house in Wellfield Road - one of the streets just off the promenade. Some eight or ten in each house, we would live there -have all our meals there and go out on parade in the street. There must have been thousands of us altogether in Blackpool. We could see all the various squads marching 'to and fro' each morning, lunchtime and evening.

As it was June/July, it was the season of holidays, but there were very few holiday makers as such and yet, as I remember it there were quite a lot of people around especially in the evenings. You can imagine us going around the 'prom' with all its seaside attractions, side shows -the Tower Ballroom, the Winter Gardens etc. There was the circus in the Tower, if I remember, but there was one snag and that was the money, as it was all very expensive. Our pay was three shillings per day and we were paid once every two weeks. That was the equivalent of fifteen new pence per day. So, on pay day, we would take one trip down the 'prom', from South Pier to North Shore and most of the pay had gone.

Blackpool did have its advantages as there was plenty to do after work. You could go to the funfair at South Shore and have a great time but like all seaside places, you needed money. When we ran out of cash we would go down to the beach and mess around for free. I do remember on many occasions, when we were in such circumstances, some of the 'either locals or holiday makers' would offer to take us for fish and chips - took pity on us I suppose.

We were to spend some months in Blackpool and we moved around from one lot of accommodation to another. I was billeted in places like Chads road and Lytham road and we worked in places like Bloomfield road football ground. I worked in offices which were in the Brighton Hydro in South Shore. I was also in several of the big hotels which people like Jack London, Peter Cane and Ernie Rodrick. They were all well known boxers who had been recruited into the RAF as physical training instructors.

I have one strange memory of this period. It was a longing to see fields and green grass again as I missed this very much, having been a 'farmer' and it was not until some considerable time later that I was to see the countryside again. It was when we went on long route marches, towards the end of our training.

We were now trained in certain aspects (drill) but we would have to go elsewhere for our trade training. For this we would be posted around the country to the various training places depending of course on the trade.

If I may refer back to my trade selection at the beginning, you will remember I was to be a Balloon Operator (Barrage Balloon) this entailed driving lorries and operating winches and as its courses were not run continuously you have to await the time for this. However, I had now finished my basic training, therefore I would leave Blackpool and as it happened the time until my course, would be spent like a lot of others, doing the menial jobs. I was therefore posted to No 5 Personnel Dispersal Centre at RAF Padgate, still in Lancashire, where I spent two enjoyable months.

The PDC was a place where RAF Airmen came to prepare for overseas postings to wherever they were required in the war zones.

I was one of the permanent staff - I emphasise this as I remember something rather sad regarding my mother. If I may explain that this period was my very first away from 'home' from Wales anyway and I suppose looking back at it now, I was rather naive, to say the least. The sadness comes from the fact that my mother kept writing letters to me but I never received them. Can you imagine a boy's mother's anguish? Her son out there somewhere in the war with no letter from him. I certainly can - even now! It was a very unnecessary misunderstanding, in that when I had given mother my address in an earlier letter, I had omitted to put 'Permanent Staff'. I should have included that in the address. The problem was that my mail had been included with the Draft Personnel who came through on their way overseas, and of course these changed weekly. It was a long time before someone realised this and eventually I received all the backlog of letters and believe it or not, a food parcel from mother, with a cake for my birthday, which by now had become inedible - sad! Not so much for me but oh for mother.

As I mentioned earlier my short stay in Padgate was a very happy one for me. I worked naturally amongst lots of other airmen and yes, airwomen. I remember my first real RAF girlfriend there and as youngsters, we got quite fond of each other, but in the services where people move around so much, nothing is permanent and the association ended when I was later posted to - guess where - back to Blackpool with the rest of the 5PDC personnel, but my girlfriend stayed at Padgate, so although I was back in Blackpool my stay was a shorted one. My trade, which I was to be trained for had changed from the original Balloon Operator to a rather obscure trade at that time - this was Plant Operator. I had been remustered by the RAF records office. The reason for this did not become clear until much later and now I can explain. A Plant Operator operates large earthmoving machines and my previous experience of working with tractors on the farm, could also be classed as earthmoving, but the RAF earth moving machines would normally be used in Airfield Construction but during the war would be used to construct temporary airstrips for our aircraft in the fighting zones.

Before I was to become a Plant Operator, I was to spend yet another short period at Stafford. Here I worked in the equipment dispatching unit and this entailed shift work. I well remember my feelings at the time as this was my first experience of working through the night. There was one thing I liked and that was at normal breakfast time when everyone else would be going to work, I would be going to bed. This job, like all the others up to now, was temporary and I was soon to be posted for my real training.

ENLISTMENT

I left the sanctuary of my lonely Welsh farm,
Where I was healthy, happy and safe from harm,
To join the men who were fighting a war,
In far off countries that I had heard of before.

I had been a farmer in a reserved occupation,
Producing the food for the rest of the nation.
They said I was needed far more on the land,
And I could do most good with a plough in my hand.

I felt like a ball about to be thrown,
Out to that far and mysterious unknown,
To sleep in a city with traffic and lights,
And barrage balloons to guard us at nights.

There were hundreds of men and company galore,
Here in the city I was lonely no more,
We travelled by train to the borders of Wales,
Out into England, from the hills to the dales.

Cont/

We were all dressed in RAF blue,
When we arrived we were told what to do.
We were issued with kit, mug, knife, fork and spoon,
And we practiced our drill both morning and noon.

Amongst the houses, hotels and domes,
We were far away from the green fields of our homes.
Not a blade of grass or a tree to be seen,
I felt a faint longing for the place where I'd been.

There were letters from home and parcels too,
From a mother who worried and cared about you.
Even in this new world that I'd found,
I hadn't forgotten how her voice would sound..

Then on the battle scarred shore of a foreign land,
I saw a native woman lead two cows in one hand.
There was not a sign of the enemy yet,
But wait! That's gunfire! How far can we get?

There is always a moment in all soldiers lives,
When they think of their homes, mothers and wives.
I was no exception though I shed not a tear,
'Cause - it was all my own fault - I did volunteer.

CHAPTER V

EARLY LIFE IN THE RAF

The Plant Training School where I was to be trained was at a place called Mill Green, near Welwyn Garden City, in Hertfordshire. My course was to last for twelve weeks. Little did I realise then that this was to be the type of work that I would be involved in for the rest of my life in the RAF and indeed, as it happened, with the construction industry after my release. I felt that I was now on my way to my future career and it gave me a feeling of importance and yes, excitement.

At Mill Green I was to find a complete change from Blackpool where we were accommodated in hotels, now it was Nissan huts. These were the hoop shaped galvanised huts which were used on the camp, built to accommodate troops during the war.

The training that we were to be involved in was not the kind that could be done anywhere as it involved very large earthmoving machines which need plenty of room and a lot of earth to 'train in'. So each day we travelled from our camp to the Plant School about four or five miles away. Early in the morning, every day, we would 'fall in threes' and be marched along the road to the school and if you can imagine marching this four or fives miles each way every day for twelve weeks you can imagine how familiar we became with all the landmarks we passed on our way. This included the Land Army Hostel, where we would always get a cheerful wave from the girls. Then there was house which we passed quite close to the road, where an elderly man stood rigidly to attention and saluted us as we marched by, regularly, he never missed. We invariably sang one of the marching songs and I may say not to the original words! I do not remember the exact months that we were there but I do know that it was summer time. We were all young lads and you can imagine sometimes when marching, if the lads in the front were in a hurry to get back, we moved at a fast pace. I remember this happening on some occasions and the corporal in charge of us would give a command to reverse the marching column, with the rear end setting the pace - happy days - yes.

Our camp, Mill Green, was situated not far from Hatfield on one side and Welwyn Garden City on the other. Our night life was mostly in Welwyn, but there were several pubs in between. I remember 'the Beehive' the 'Pear Tree' and in Welwyn itself, the 'Cherry Tree'. Welwyn was in those days a 'garden city' and it was something new as towns went - modern I suppose. There was also another pub I remember called the 'Green Man', this was nearer Hatfield town.

Although we did not realise it at the time, we were to spend some considerable time at Mill Green, for after our twelve weeks at the school we were to form a new Plant Unit and it was all towards the war effort -it was very tough training in both trade and, most important, physical fitness. Maybe at this stage I should try and relate to some of the other members of the Plant Flight. When we were brought together here at Mill Green, and, as it transpired, we were to remain together for the duration of the war on the continent, although we did not realise it at that time.

We were a fair cross section of young men and older experienced men, from various parts of the country. We had the Jocks' the 'Taffs' the 'Geordies' and 'Scousers' etc. As a Welshman I was naturally a 'Taff' and I have remained so to this day by any of these people who have a reason to refer to me, even now.

We were all soon to become very familiar with the activities and we got to know each other very well. In this kind of unit, it is most important that this (esprit de corps) exists as who knows, some day one may depend on your colleagues when in danger.

I must now mention my Welsh friend Tommy Jones - he originated from the same part of Wales that I did, although I did not know him previously. We became very close and whenever possible we spoke Welsh to each other. Unfortunately as we were in the midst of English speaking men, we found that they were very suspicious of Tom and myself - they thought that we were talking about them! But of course we were not.

During the next few months at Mill Green, we were to be subjected to many arduous and difficult tasks, the purpose of which was to train and test our ability, fitness and eventually our efficiency as a unit. This was exactly what I wanted to do, as we were put through our paces every day. I remember the three mile runs, and the twenty mile route marches very well. On frosty morning, very early, before the local population were up, we would go marching along the road, even before the white hoar frost had risen. I was well prepared for this, as I had lived and worked on the farm all my life. Towards the end of our training at Mill Green, when we had been equipped with our Plant Machines and these ranged from big bulldozers to heavy excavators and all the machines we would require to carry out our work later on. And eventually all the heavy transport required to become fully mobile. We carried out several full scale exercises. These entailed written instructions which were handed to our Commanding Officer, with instructions not to open the sealed orders until maybe 02.00 hours as we knew it and the orders would state that we were to load up all our equipment machines and all and be outside the camp gate before 0.4.00 hours, on our way to destinations such as Paisley near Glasgow, Quay near Cambridge and we also had one to Bristol. The purpose was of course to test our ability to move at very short notice. I remember on one such convoy, this was to Paisley, our journey took us through Doncaster, where we staged an overnight stay. As the intention was to get us used to living rough, we were detailed to sleep on the terraces of the grandstand at Doncaster Race Course. So, imagine if you can, about a hundred men all sleeping on the terraces, each one rolled up in his bedding, mostly with their heads covered, as it was cold by this time. However, why I recollect this particular night, is that I had been detailed, along with others, to do convoy guard. Guard duties in the services are normally two hours on and four hours off. This meant that after two hours we were to awaken the next two to replace us.

Normally this would have been fairly easy, but can you imagine trying to find two particular lads amongst the hundred - in the dark, with blankets over their heads! Well, it was not so much finding the two, as dealing with the abuse we received from the wrong ones, who, quite rightly I suppose, were rather annoyed at being woken up unnecessarily. Needless to say by the time we found them, their duty time had expired.

This kind of toughening up training was to continue for some considerable time and as a result we became very fit and our practical work with the machines contributed to the high standard that would be required of us in the future -we all hoped that this future was not too far away. We were all fairly young men, twenties to thirties but there were also some men with 'civvie street' experience; they must have been forty or maybe a few were even fifty - very old men as far as we were concerned then! We were by now a fully manned unit and it seemed that we were destined to be together for a long time. We trained together, we lived together and we all socialised, if one could call it that. In the services ones spare time or time off depended entirely on the activities. We were told at the beginning that we were on duty for twenty three hours and fifty nine minutes a day. We were, I believe one of the first organizations to use the twenty four hour system. It seems that whoever devised the system did not account for the very last minute i.e. one minute to twelve. So, if we were out at night on a pass or on leave our time for return was usually 23.59 hours on a certain day. We became eventually so well trained in fact, that it was well known that should there be an emergency or special requirement, we were inevitably called upon to do the necessary.

I well remember one evening, it was by now, winter time, just after we had had our evening meal, there was a roar of aircraft and suddenly, out of the dark sky we made out the shape of a large bomber flying so low that it seemed that it could no longer continue but is passed over the camp and it was assumed that it must have crashed not too far away. We were then told that it was a German bomber that had been shot down. So we were instructed to report to our place of duty and we were in a very short time on board transport heading for the German bomber. We were all geared up to capture the German 'baddies' - can you imagine our excitement, but alas, when we arrived we discovered that the bomber was one of our own bombers and we never did find out how it had been shot down.

This of course had been some very important training for us, even though it had been a false alarm. It had at least exercised our ability to locate a given target. This exercise was made easier due to the fact that we had, on several occasions been on night exercises where we would be taken out in the middle of the night, driven around, so as to disorientate us, then we would be dropped off many miles away from our camp and told to find our way back. This was of course to all of us young ones, great fun. I remember going along merrily in the dark, across some fields and I was suddenly confronted by a high netting wire fence, so I turned and went in the other direction, only to find the same problem. It was a while before we discovered that we had entered a very large wire mesh compound. On this occasion we arrived back at camp in time for an early breakfast and then to work.

After a few more weeks and a few more exercises our time at Hatfield was drawing to a close and we were to move, along with other units, to form what was to be our Airfield Construction Squadron - formed 1st March, 1944- 5022 Squadron. The location for the formation was at or near a placed called Elstead in Surrey. There was believe it or not, still further training but this time as part of a far larger unit - a complete squadron.

Our actual location was on a common with various wooded areas, where we would hide our transport and plant machines and we found that there was no permanent accommodation. We slept in tents and our meals were cooked and served in the open. We did have a marquee to eat our meals in. The weather by now was improving and it was 'spring'. We were subjected to 'roughing it' in that the toilets we had were just holes in the ground with poles across to sit on, maybe I should have said 'rails'. I just thought it would be rather awkward doing it on a 'pole'. For washing and shaving we had to walk about one hundred yards to a stream - here we would wash and shave using little mirrors, wedged or hanging from a twig, many of these were pieces of broken mirrors.

Out of all this there was, believe it or not a 'bright spot' in the way of the village pub, where most of us ended up, at night. The pub was a typical 'village pub' with limited accommodation, consequently most of us ended up sitting outside at small tables. There was a problem as there were so many of us, there were insufficient beer vessels to go around. Therefore it was usually the first in, first served and if you had a glass then you hung on to it. By the end of the evening we would all be at least 'happy' and I remember on one or two occasions we would all form up in a column and march back to camp with a Scotsman by the name of Jock McPhee at the head leading us to a good old Scottish tune on his bagpipes. Needless to say we were not very popular with the locals or indeed with our officers when we reached camp.

We had now been training for many months and we were gradually becoming a part of a larger unit. We would still be taking part in various exercises, like one I remember. I was taken with my machine, by low loader and trailer to Southampton. The problem in those days was that you were told very little or as little as possible - so, I arrived at Southampton and it turned out that I was to be loaded on to a LST (Landing Ship Tanks). I, along with many others, drove up the steep ramps into the bowels of the strange vessel, still not knowing where were going to. So, we sailed and when it was night time we all went to our beds on the upper level, while the transport and machines were safely anchored on the lower deck.

In the middle of the night, when we were all asleep, there was a terrible commotion. I woke up to hear the emergency siren blaring away, which meant that there was some kind of emergency or danger. Bearing in mind that there was a war on and that we were now out on the open sea, the first thought that comes to mind is to escape to safety. It was possible that we were in danger or even sinking, but wait for it, the message that came over the tannoy said that we were all to go down below to where the vehicles were stored and remain there. But if you take the old favourite saying 'ours is not to reason why - we are here to do or die'. It was such a relief when a further message was broadcast to say that the exercise was now over and that we could return to our beds. Can you imagine what some of the boys were saying and calling the authorities. However, as far as I was concerned it was another bit of experience.

Later on we came back to land, somewhere in Devon and I remember when the transport that had taken me to Southampton was waiting for me in Devon. We then travelled back to Elstead in Surrey. I remember seeing and being very impressed with Torquay and the South of England.

I think that with all these various training exercises we were becoming reasonably confident and of course we thought that we could cope with almost any problem.

There was one further exercise that I remember, it was to do with the 'buzz bombs' or 'doodle bugs' as they were called. The war had been going for some time and Germany had managed to get through the 'Maginot Line' (this was the defence line made by the French, to keep the Germans out) and the Germans had taken France and arrived at Calais on the coast. We were, I must say, not involved in that episode, but back to our exercise in the South of England.

Germany had developed the first unmanned missile. It was referred to as the V one and while it was to all intents and purposes a bomb, it had an engine and could therefore be launched and directed at targets in England. The method of hitting the target was governed by the amount of fuel. When it ran out of fuel it came down and exploded on impact. The air defence - the anti-aircraft guns - would try and shoot down these objects and were sometimes successful, but most reached their destinations.

Our part in this was in the South of England, an area which the missiles would be passing over. Our job was to make 'barrage balloon' sites, to try and obstruct some of the missiles and bring them down. For the purpose of these exercises we were based at RAF Biggin Hill and we went out daily in the morning and returned at night. This kind of work was useful experience. We were authorised to go on to farmers' land and work on the jobs without even asking the poor farmers. I can only remember one farmer that protested and he was most annoyed.

While we had been involved in all these various exercises there had been a lot of talk of the 'second front'. This was to be an attack on the continent so as to relieve the pressure on the poor Russians who had been fighting the Germans all though the winter and up to June. So it was not surprising that everything seemed to be geared towards that end.

After we had returned to Elstead, our base, we got up one morning to see some of our aircraft flying over and these had been painted in strange black and white stripes and we soon discovered that this was because, we the British, had actually landed in France and the 'second

front' was under way. This was known as 'D' Day. Our departure to the battle zone became more imminent by the day and everyone was ready and keen to go. As the time grew nearer we were put on standby which gradually decreased from twenty four hours to eventually, hourly.

CHAPTER VI

WAR IN EUROPE

At last the time came for us to move out and on that fine morning on the 9thJuly, 1944, we sat in our vehicles and waved goodbye to those we left behind, looking into the mysterious future, bound for Normandy.

When we moved now, it was to take all the Plant Transport and all our working equipment with us. We had a light convoy of dozens of lorries carrying personnel and then we had the heavy convoy which conveyed all the heavy 20 ton bulldozers, scrapers and all earth moving equipment. These two convoys travelled to Southampton to be loaded onto the special landing ships, which would take us across the channel. These ships were flat bottomed, single deck open types and were designed to sail as far as possible into the shore, where the large end ramp would provide protection from enemy fire, until they would be lowered to allow the vehicles to travel off the deck, down into the water, which could be many feet deep. Most of the vehicles had been water-proofed to overcome the water. There were several of these ships needed to carry all our equipment and I well remember the feeling of leaving the shores of England. Our crossing was done during the night, and of course in total darkness as to show a light would have invited trouble from the enemy.

For most of the journey all went well, quietly and peacefully, but I do remember being aroused from sleep by a tremendous 'bang' which shook the whole ship. It was most frightening, when you think that we were going to war anyway. It turned out that we were only two thirds of the way across the channel and in the dark and the mist, our boat and another one had actually collided, and the 'bang' was the result of the two metal hulls colliding. Fortunately there was no damage and we carried on to our destination. When a little later, it dawned, we saw in the light of day - the sea - which I remember was so calm, calmer I think than a duck pond! The surface even appeared glassy.

We were destined to go ashore on 'Juno' beach head. All the various beaches had been given different code names. As we approached the coast of France we all prepared ourselves and our machines for a fast getaway as soon as the ramp went down. Looking at the coast on our approach, we saw what had been a pleasant coastline, but now it was a brown mass of shell holes. This was the result of the tremendous barrage that had been directed at the defences prior to the first landing and something I shall never forget, I saw a lonely woman leading two cows on a rope.

Then came the moment when the boat charged the beach head and we heard and felt the bottom strike the shore and then, immediately the big end ramp, which had sheltered us, was lowered with a splash and part of it disappeared under the water. This was 'it', this was our entrance into the Second Front.

We were all driving either plant machines or transporters, so we quickly disembarked. I was driving my machine – I remember the feeling of driving into the water, not knowing how deep it was. The reason for all the urgency apparently was that although the artillery from the shore had been silenced, the Germand were continually making raids with their dive bombers, especially looking for landings, so we were quickly marshalled ashore to more obscure areas.

We were now ashore. I remember I was proud to be part of the Second Front. We were then to make our first journey on French soil, through cornfields, over dusty tank tracks. We were suddenly aware of the smell of battle. This was partly due to the dozens of dead animals, mainly cows. I shall never forget the first sight of the fallen German soldiers. Most had been buried in very shallow graves but some had

LA BATAILLE DE NORMANDIE

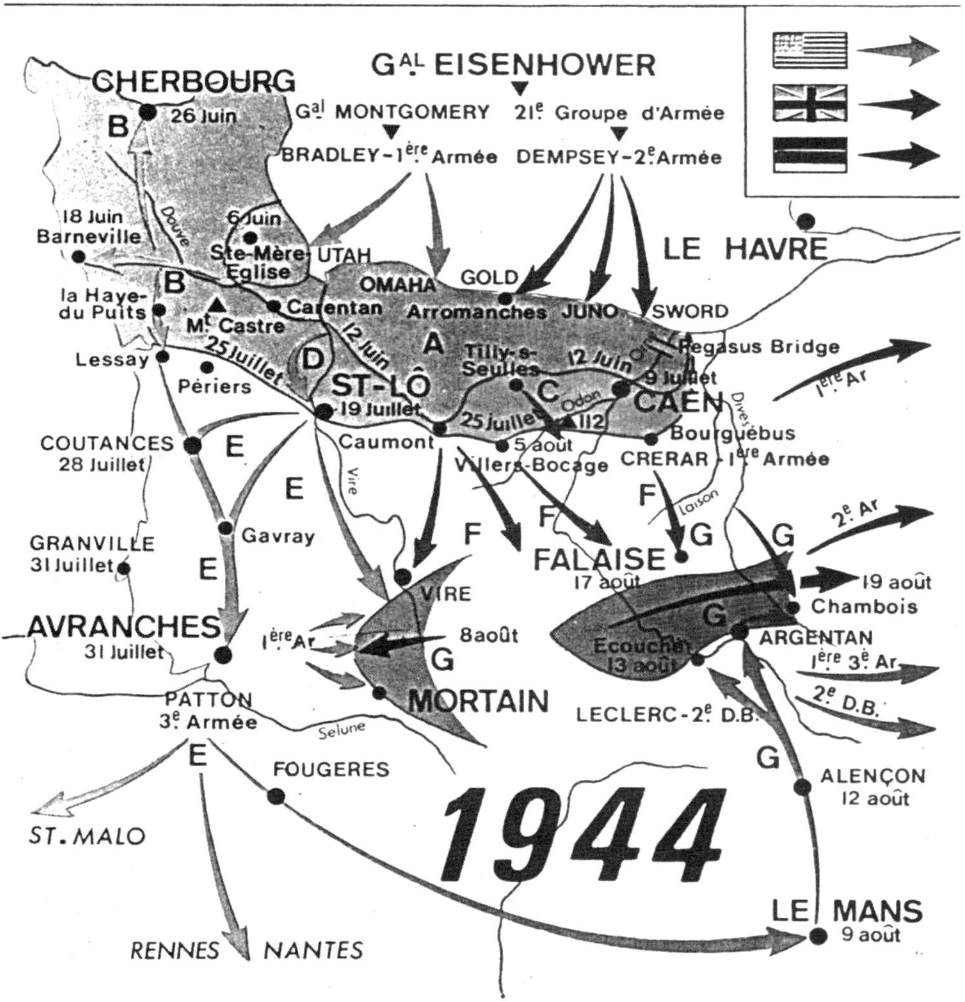

THE BATTLE ZONE

Our landing craft charged the shore
Into the sand until it could go no more.
When the ramp is lowered down
It's into the sea to float or drown.

Then the joy to feel your feet on solid sand
Even though it is part of a foreign land
The water now is not so deep,
As we follow our leader in his jeep.

There are signs of those that have gone before,
Some no further than this shore.
All those crosses scattered around
Each marks a body in the ground.
It seems for now their day is done,
Each and all some mothers' son.

We are now in the battle zone
Where life is cheap and we are not alone.
We are legitimate targets for the foe
Seeking shelter in the trench below.

But we are not here to hide away,
We have come to fight and are here to stay.
Although the enemy is out of sight,
The gunfire proves he's there alright

We then advance to our next destination,
Following a trail of death and destruction.
The cattle in the fields are lying prostrate,
Through no fault of their own, they suffered this fate.

Continued

It is summer and in the heat of the day
There is a horrid smell of flesh in decay.
'This is normal for war', that's what we're told
How could we know? We're not that old

A soldier is a man with fear in his heart,
He is therefore a fighter, right from the start
'Attack', they say, is his best means of defence,
Where courage prevails o'er all common sense.

A soldier is conditioned to suffer his sorrow.
Maybe, surviving today to fight for tomorrow.
At the end of the day - if he's still alive!
He will have to fight again just to survive.

Each day seems to start from yesterday's battle,
From the destruction, the killing and all those dead cattle.
But we that are left must fight on again,
To ensure the fallen did not die in vain.

---

not been completely covered. There was also British graves - all temporary, with some kind of marker, either a rough wooden cross or even a rifle sticking in the ground. The steel helmet was always placed on the cross and this was either the British or German type. Some of the crosses had names roughly written on pieces of paper or a card, all really 'some mother's son'.

We were soon to become familiar with these conditions. As we travelled a little further inland, there were definite tracks to follow and if we went on to a road, the verges were still mined. Then, when the excitement of landing had died down, we were suddenly aware of gun fire in the distance and this made me conscious of my safety, but I was not really afraid (too young I suppose). As we travelled in small units, one of our flights travelled towards Caen, then a battle ground, but soon made a speedy return and then there were some rounds of shells from the German artillery, but no casualties. The whole area around was a mass of trenches where our boys and the Canadians had fought their way from the beach head.

We eventually reached a position as far forward as it was safe to go and it was here that we were to stay for a short while. It was a place, just a place in a field. We were as a unit, self supporting. We had tents for accommodation, water was carried in the water bowser and food consisted of a 24 hour pack, which we had been issued with. This pack contained concentrated food, mostly in cubes. We had porridge, hard tack biscuits, veg, tea and a big bar of chocolate. This was also in concentrated form and probably, most important, you had the printed instructions on how to share out the various meals, like breakfast, lunch etc. I well remember the instruction regarding the chocolate - break off small pieces and chew until it was in a state to be swallowed. It did not really taste like chocolate, but it did have the goodness.

On our first night we had 'dug in', this was the only safe way to live. We had excavated a square hole in the ground; slightly less in size than the tent and then placed the tent over it. We were fortunate in that we had the earth moving digger to do the digging. We would then sleep in the bottom of the 'pit'; conditions were such that we would also dig a hole into the side of the first excavation and wearing a steel helmet lie with ones head in the hole. This might sound rather drastic but we were soon to experience the real conditions.

First of all, our Naval warships were firing shells over our heads towards the German positions and the Germans were firing in return on our Navy. Although this was not directed at us, it was very disturbing to hear the guns firing and the shells whizzing overhead.

We had, for reasons of protection, parked our transport and machines around the field, close to or under hedges, with camouflage nets to hide it from the air. In addition to the ship to shore shelling we had dawn and dusk raids by enemy aircraft dropping anti-personnel bombs. These bombs were equipped with a long stem which contacted the ground and detonated the bomb several feet above the ground. The effect was that shrapnel was scattered to cause the maximum damage and injury. It was very effective as damage was caused in the way of broken windscreens and some of the bits went straight through our tents.

I remember our first morning in France, we were, we discovered, not far from Bretville. For our breakfast, our Warrant Officer collected all our porridge cubes to cook them in one pot and we all shared the meal. We were not totally unprepared for this, for it you remember, our training at Elstead, although this now seemed so far away (and safe) so we were not disappointed when we had to go with our mess tin in hand for our very little breakfast.

As it was not possible to move very far, our work was very local and we soon were working for real. We helped the Royal Engineers build a new road at Tilly. Bretville was not a large town. I know that it had a church with a spire or it had had a spire! It had been hit by shells and was just about half its size. Bretville was a hive of industry with all the transport taking up supplies to our forward positions and in return convoys of ambulances bringing back our wounded soldiers and possibly our dead. When I was going through one day, I saw most of the traffic brought to a standstill to allow our Prime Minister, Mr Churchill with his motor bike outriders come through, the stopped traffic included the line of ambulances carrying the wounded.

This then was my introduction to the war and I felt at times that I wished I was back on the farm in Wales. I could have been, as I had a choice, but this feeling was only temporary - for being young and adventurous and amongst all your comrades one soon forgets these feelings and become familiar with most situations. For people that are not or have not been involved in these situations, you may think how horrible for soldiers to have to go up to the front and fight, yes, but I can say after seeing soldiers of various nationalities, coming and going 'up front', that you do get 'seasoned' gradually, starting from the training, through various stages. I suppose getting acclimatised would be the word.

It was by now, summer, and as the weather was warm and dry, conditions were very dusty and it caused the smell of decay - mainly from dead cows and even human bodies.

I have vivid memories of night stops in France. As we always travelled in our respective vehicles with our machines on trailers, depending on circumstances, we would try and stay overnight in some sheltered spot if we could otherwise we would try and get below ground. We would sleep sometimes under the heavy trailers. So, with your kit, usually for me it was kept in a metal box, which had been previously used for ammunition, you would take off your boots and take a blanket in under the very low trailer.

It was from one of these situations that I woke up to feel the rain, which was seeping through the trailer on to my face. I remember I turned over and the next time I awoke it was morning and it was still raining very hard. When I got out from beneath the trailer I was very wet and when I went to put on my boots, I remember they were full of water. So, after taking off my clothes and donning my greatcoat, I plunged my feet into the wet boots and plodded to where we were to have our breakfast, passing on the way, dozens of dead cows. We later retrieved the situation somewhat by gathering firewood from the hedges and making a very big bonfire - the heat of this did dry our clothes out.

B19 Lingevres 31st July - We were an Airfield Construction Unit and this was the .function for which we had come. As the front line moved slowly and the allies won more of France, we were ready and poised to do the job which we had been trained for constructing temporary airstrips in the forward battle area, so that our fighter aircraft could operate to give the ground troops support. Our first opportunity came on the 31st July, when we were instructed to move forward to an area where we constructed our first airstrip. These were all eventually given code numbers and this one was to be 'B19'. This was near a place called Lingevres in Normandy. The area was mostly cornfields and, believe it or not, we helped the farmers when they tried to salvage as much as possible of their crops. All our work, like everyone up front was urgent, as our fighter aircraft were badly in need of somewhere to operate from and as the front line was continually advancing, so would be the requirement for more fresh airstrips. It is on record to say that a thousand men worked on the airstrip from 07.00 hours, (seven o'clock in the morning) to 11.00 hours (eleven o'clock at night), until the airstrip was ready on the 8th August - a little more than a week. The first Spitfire landed. A little later a squadron of Typhoons came and used the strip continuously. After such a concentrated period of work, one looks for a little respite.

Colombier 12th August - On the 12th August we were on the move forward to a location known as Colombier. Here we were to construct an advanced landing ground for Auster light aircraft for General Montgomery.

I well remember this as I was one of the bulldozer operators involved. The plan was to remove the hedges between three small field to allow the aircraft to use the whole length for landing and taking off.

What I remember of this, is that General Montgomery also had a larger Dakota Aircraft which he used and we discovered that the pilot of this had a bet that he could land and take off on that very small strip. Well, we were soon to find out, for as soon as we had finished, sure enough here comes the Dakota down close to one end and it pulled up and stopped in plenty of time, but - now came the test as the Dakota is a fair size and the strip was small. To take off, the pilot took it as close as possible to one end, so that it had as much room as possible for the take off. He then carried out his preparation and started his run up the strip. Bearing in mind that we had removed two hedges and this had left slight 'dips'. Well, when the aircraft came up the strip he hit the dip, bounced into the air and did not come down! So he had used only two thirds of the distance and had got away with it.

Conde 16th August. On the 16th August we were again on the move, always forward with the front. We were to go to a place or town called Conde. Conde was originally a town, but now it was only a mountain of brick and rubble. The fighting around here had been hard and difficult, as the place had the advantage of a very important bridge across a river and as it was important, the Germans had defended it fiercely. There was a sickly smell about the place. There were fields littered with dead animals and the bodies of the fallen, slung into ditches in the heat of the battle, these were covered with just a few inches of soil.

The town had been bombed by the allies in the night and it had been reduced to rubble and on the following day the American bombers had also bombed the ruins. Our task was to clear a way through the town, find the roads and reach the bridge; clearing a way for our tanks and armour to pass through.

The German army was not far away and the bridge was by no means ours yet. However, while we were digging our way through the rubble, some Germans managed to blow up the bridge and we were to see our first German prisoners. They came and gave themselves up, as they were the remnants of the fierce battle which had now moved forward.

I have other memories of Conde. When bulldozing the way through the rubble we came across strange sights. At one time I was surrounded by bottles of wine, spirits and others. I had entered what remained of a cellar. There was also a cellar full of coal. We finished the job and we were once more on the move.

Movement up through France was strictly controlled as the tank tracks and the road, when we used them, were continuously packed with vehicles of all descriptions, from tanks to ambulances according to priority. One most important kind of traffic was the convoys of British prisoners of war that had been released. On one occasion, I cannot remember exactly where, near a place called Forges. Our long convoy had to pass another long convoy of prisoners on their way home. The roads at that time were straight and tree lined, but oh so narrow. So you can imagine two convoys passing each other. I was travelling in a heavy vehicle with a trailer, on which I had my bulldozer, and as we pulled in to try and allow the prisoners by, our vehicle got stuck and in trying to get out the bulldozer slowly rolled over and down into the field below. The Warrant Officer came along the line and told me and a mate Johnny Shotton, to stay with the machine until we would be picked up later. When left to our own devices we discovered a fairly new wooden shed which was unoccupied, so we chose to sleep in it.

We had been given a few tins of bully beef and a pack of biscuits. We were quite near a small village and we found a small cafe and for our tin of bully beef and a packet of cigarettes, we had a fair meal.

The fighting around Normandy had been hard and fierce, as the Germans had resisted strongly. But now it seemed one could feel that things were moving. It was written of this phase 'the great advance was now on'. The allies, both American and British, with 'Monty' as General Commanding the British Army, had made advances and had so we thought, surrounded thousands of Germans in the 'Falaise Gap'. But when the net closed, there were not so many Germans there. So, as we advanced forward, through the 'Falaise Gap', we were the first British troops that the French had seen.

24th August - Gace. After our work at Conde, with its terrible 'stink of death', we were very glad to move to this rather quieter area. We erected our tents in an orchard, but we had by now realised that it was never safe to live or sleep at ground level. So we would automatically 'dig in', but it seemed that we had some respite from the incessant shelling.

We were soon to move forward once more. This is how we moved up through France, make a strip for forward aircraft, but this only lasted as long as the front line was near. We were now becoming familiar with the drill. The countryside was war scarred and the population had either moved forward or rearward, until it was safe to return.

We found ruins in most towns and villages and even farms. We would usually go through the contents of the buildings, picking up bits and pieces, like radios etc. We would also be on the lookout for food, as we were living on 'hard tack', mostly tins, like bully beef and biscuits. The biscuits were hard concentrated material and difficult to eat.

I remember one day, we went into a farmyard and we saw mostly dead animals but we saw a cockerel running around, so we thought of catching and having it for the pot. So we chased it around for a while. I had caught chickens this way before, but after a while the cock ran into a shed. I followed feeling that I had it cornered, but - oh inside was a dead cow; it had been dead for a few days and the stink was awful, the cock ran behind it and we were forced to leave it there as we could not stand the stench.

I do remember a similar exercise when we were successful and we took the chicken back to our camp, somewhere along a hedge and as we were cooking it in a pot, our officer passed by and his only remark was 'bully beef and biscuits'? Sarcastically!

As we progressed through France from one airstrip to another, we found that we sometimes made our camps in orchards or other suitable corners where there was cover, but always below ground level. I remember on one of these stops we were up with the forward guns. The artillery had eight heavy guns quite near to us and when they fired, it was usual to put up a barge. One would start and the others would follow and at that particular time, I remember, at night the Germans were also firing in our direction. So, lying below ground we would hear the German gunfire and then just when you would expect their shells to land there would be an almighty bang, as the gun nearest to us would fire. But, believe it or not, like the gunners in their pits, we would sleep through most of it.

I remember doing guard duty at night, always in pairs. At times we would have to spend most of the time on the edge of a 'slit trench' so that we could dive in if it got too 'hot'.

It was now late summer and were heading in the direction of Belgium - towards Amiens. The weather was dry and the dust was rising wherever there was any movement, especially on the tank tracks where you could hear the dull rumble of tanks. The tank tracks were tracks made through fields, in a direct line and probably safer than the narrow road, where all the verges were mined anyway. Our presence up front was considered to be important enough to allow us to use the tank track. There was a saying - something like: I forget the beginning but it went - 'Something, something in God we trust, but Gerry shoots, at a cloud of dust'.

We were advancing fast and approaching Brussels at the beginning of September, arriving at Amiens on the 2nd September. As we travelled through the town and villages, we were greeted by the inhabitants, lined up, to cheer our arrival. This was a welcome sight for us as opposed to the villages that we had passed through previously, just piles of brick rubble. The scenery depended on the fierceness of the fighting -we were soon to pass this part, as very soon the front of our hundred vehicle convoy was entering a war torn valley, where the battle had wrecked every building and crushed the wood to splinters, and killed every living animal. It was a sad sight, as you saw the odd peasant searching amongst the rubble - for what? Or maybe, for whom? The white crosses along the road were always an indication of the fierceness of the fighting that had taken place.

There were a few shots of small arms fire from the nearby shattered woods - this was always an indication of our relationship to the front line and the fighting, which was now making massive surge forward at a good rate. So, at Amiens, we were there only long enough to make a grass strip alongside the main runway and this took just one good long day and at the end we were to see over a hundred Typhoons land the same day. Our work was continuous - the sooner we finished one job the sooner we were to start another. So again, one echelon was to remain to repair the main runway (these had in nearly every instance been sabotaged by the Germans), the other echelon had instructions to move, always forward, to Lille. Our job at Lille was as usual to repair, this time the concrete runway. There was as usual many dozens of bomb craters to repair.

Our next move took us into and through Brussels in Belgium. This trip I shall never forget - the welcome we received, was to say the least, tremendous. It became difficult to proceed due to the people who were showering goodies on us, including drinks of all kinds. However, we eventually got through and we were once more moving forward, this time to Burg-Leopald, where we had to wait as we were now up near the front line and things were getting a bit hot.

We were not able to go any further, until the army had crossed the Escaut and Albert canals. The Guards Armoured Brigade was up ahead of us. We ended up on a site not far from Diest and my main memory of this stage was a job that we had later on. It was to do once more with the V(I) and the V(II) - the V ones and the V twos - these were what we referred to earlier as the Doodle-bugs or Buzz Bombs. We were once more to prepare some artillery and balloon sites to deter or impede their path to the UK - London. We were to work initially in Diest, a place which had been badly bombed and we were to use the resulting debris to make roads and hard-standing for the site at Louvene.

Although the majority of the buildings had been reduced to rubble, I remember, there was of all places, a cafe or as we would say, a pub, still standing. I remember this because we went in each day to eat our rations. I have to this day, a silver coin; a pre-war Belgian 50 franc piece, which the lady of the house gave me.

Most of the squadron had to wait a little longer before we could make a move to Holland, towards Eindhoven. At one point we came to a halt as the road had been cut by the Germans. I remember having to sleep with my rifle fully loaded and safety catch off, alongside me in 'bed'. We eventually reached Eindhoven; this was very important strategically and little did we know at the time that we were to spend a longer period here than anywhere we had been. Eindhoven Airfield had been badly treated by all concerned. The Germans had bombed the runway, and there were about one hundred and fifty bomb craters to be filled in and I remember the grass strips alongside the runway had been zig-zagged with a plough to stop aircraft landing on it. Our job, as usual, was to provide landing and take off facilities as soon as possible.

During the German occupation, the local Dutch people had been forced to work on the maintenance of the airfield and they had consequently sabotaged the drainage systems, a feature so important in Holland's low lying lands. It was now September, and the summer was drawing to a close. The work was to get more and more difficult. The fighting was now getting nearer to Germany, hence the stiffer resistance and the rate of advance was slowing down.

We have I suppose more memories of Eindhoven than other places which were passed through swiftly as our stay was a considerably long one and we were to experience the very cold and hard winter, but I shall never forget the men of Arnhem. We saw wave after wave of Dakotas towing gliders and from my vantage point in the top of a Dutch windmill, I saw many hundreds of gliders cut loose to land in the surrounding countryside. We later saw many of these in the most strange places and positions, in gardens, in woods and some even in trees. We were after all in a narrow corridor from Eindhoven to Niemegen and Arnhem, anyone who has been privileged to read 'The Men of Arnhem - The Red Berets' will be aware of the most fiercely fought battle. Our airborne boys had been 'dropped' into Arnhem, to capture several important bridges before the Germans blew them up, but the Germans were aware of the attempts and were waiting for them. The paratroopers were surrounded and had to fight their way out, suffering serious losses. The corridor in which we found ourselves was narrow and the Germans in their attempt to recover it did on several occasions, cut it in different places, so we were always on the alert, especially at night time. This was another occasion when we had strange 'bed mates' in the way of our rifles, which were loaded for immediate use, under the blanket.

After our initial period at Einhoven, when we carried out the initial and emergency repair to the runways, including the grass strips parallel to the main runway, we had the task of carrying out more permanent repairs to the main concrete runway. We would as a rule, be able to provide landing and take off facilities in the first few days and this was no exception. We were able to have the grass strip ready and we saw the dozens of Typhoons landing and taking off on their bombing circuits on enemy lines. We were to spend several months at Eindhoven and the front line was never very far away. At one time the Typhoon would take off in one direction, drop their bombs on the enemy and come and land again, all in one circuit - this must have been the shortest 'sortie' on record.

The winter was with us and the weather got colder, making our work of repairing the damaged airfield more and more difficult. Our works Flights were engaged in repairing the bomb craters on the runway, using concrete and the frost was a problem. It slowed down the work and even stopped it for short periods. My involvement was as always as a machine operator; so that kind of work went on as we got involved in snow clearing and removing the ice from the runway. But we had our own problems, in that our machines would freeze up and as antifreeze liquid was not available at that time we had to drain our cooling systems every evening and refill each morning. Some of the Flights worked on night shift, and we always had the guard to watch over the plant at night. One memory remains with me to this day. On this particular morning we were on the transport travelling to the far end of the airfield, and as it was very cold and frosty, I did not look forward to getting the cold water – if it was not frozen - and filling up my radiator. But what I remember is, as we approached our parking area, the guard had lit a tremendous fire of wood, which had been gathered and around it were dozens of jerricans filled with water for our rads and of course the fire also kept the frost from our machines.

OUR POSITION AT EINDHOVEN DURING THE BATTLE FOR ARNHEIM

The previous episode reminds me of another involving jerricans. There must have been millions of these around the continent as all the fuel for use in the forward area was received in these. Even the fuel for aircraft and if I can point out that normal petrol for road going vehicles was also in jerricans. The only difference was that the vehicle petrol was eighty octane and the aircraft fuel was a hundred octane which meant a higher flashpoint. The jerrican, when emptied of fuel was used for many purposes including carrying water for various uses, such as for filling radiators etc. We would also carry water in these for washing hands and eating utensils.

Where we were based for our work on the airfield, we had the use of a Nissan hut to shelter in and we would probably eat our midday rations in there and not unlike many other situations we had a fire inside contained in a forty gallon drum, which burned long pieces of wood, collected for that purpose and to take advantage of the heat, we would place a jerry can full of water across the top of the fire so that the flames could quickly warm the water.

It was to this situation that I walked into the hut - the fire - and twenty or thirty men sitting around warming themselves in the short break that they had for tea. I noticed the jerry can engulfed in the leaping flames, with the top end towards me and I was horrified as I realised that the seal of the opening was still intact. This meant one thing -the jerry can contained four and half gallons of 100 octane aircraft fuel (petrol) and I noticed further that the sides of the can had already swollen out. It was I thought, about ready to explode. I grabbed a bar from nearby, pushed it through the handle of the can and shouted to someone to grab the other end and in one move we lifted the can, carried it out through the door, dumped it on the ground and ran for our lives. I hate to think of the consequences if we had not removed the can, most of the men were around the fire and within a few feet of it. I do not remember anyone saying 'thank you' or even mentioning it after that. I suppose that living in the conditions that existed around then, with shells and bombs, this little episode did not seem too different.

We had been in Eindhoven for longer than any other place. The reason was that the Germans were putting up a stiffer resistance. In November the German Army made an attempt to break through the American lines in the region known as the Ardennes. They were

successful in breaching the front line and made a spearhead into Belgium. For some days they advanced and seemed to be making for the port of Antwetp in Holland. It so happened that the weather was so cloudy this and the accompanying mist prevented our aircraft from taking part. So the advance went on for about a week, this was when we were moved back to Diest.

To counteract the German offensive some of the British tanks were brought back from the front - the road and tracks were a continuous line of tanks travelling from North to South from the direction of Arnhem towards France, and as they were heading back the way that we had come, the locals I remember, remarked that we were all going home again. What was really happening was that the 'Allies' were preparing a 'pincer' movement with attacks from either side of the long German 'corridor' and cut it off and it was then surrounded and that was the end of the Ardennes offensive.

December found us still in Eindhoven as there was very little movement up front. I for one, will never forget the winter - it was hard and cold. We were reasonably established at Eindhoven, indeed some of the boys were very well established as they had found some of the local girls and frequented their homes, with all the comforts.

I have many memories of the place. It was above all low lying - wet-cold, but more peaceful than the other places we had visited. I remember we ate all our meals in some sort of building and our food consisted mainly of tinned materials. When we had breakfast we had tinned bacon in slices and some of the boys would leave the rind and there was a little girl that came every morning to collect the rinds and placed them carefully in a paper bag - as far as I know the scraps were for human consumption.

We were now well into the winter and we were to spend Christmas here. There was not a lot of difference in the Christmas dinner and other dinners, except for the spirit. I think it made us all think more of home maybe. So Christmas came and went and we were to see a new year starting.

Oh, but what a new year - New Years Day at Eindhoven will never be forgotten by any of the people who were there on that day. We had all started work and it was about ten o'clock in the morning if I remember. We had not seen any German aircraft for about two months. I was standing just outside the workshops as my machine was in for servicing. I heard the sound of aircraft flying at tree top height and saw several aircraft which I thought at first were ours, but now I could see the markings were distinctly German and from then on all hell let loose at the first burst of cannon shells - I dived into the inspection pit, now there were more aircraft and they were flying up and down the airfield firing at anything and everything including the aircraft parked on the dispersal. There was a large column of black smoke coming from the fuel dump which had been hit; there were explosions from the direction of the bomb dump. Our own fighter aircraft were prevented from taking off as they were fired on as soon as they appeared on the runway.

Two of our pilots tried to take off in their Typhoons on the perimeter track, they were fired on - both collided with each other and both hit a barrack hut. Everything caught fire and the dead pilots were still in the burnt out cockpits the next day. Although there were not many deaths, there was a lot of damage.

When I thought that the aircraft had left I went out for a look and just as if it had been waiting for me, was this German pilot in his low flying aircraft. I actually saw the pilot as he swooped and turned and fired his cannon. His shells were hitting the concrete all around me. I dived for cover once more and then it seemed that it was all quiet again - they had gone. I realised later that this was a suicide attack as the Germans attacked all our airfields at the same moment, so that one could not come to the assistance of the others. Our own Typhoons from Eindhoven were at that time out on a raid, but they returned and between them, and the fighter escort of our bombers from England, they shot all the German raiders down - yes that was a 'Happy New Year'.

During the winter months, we had a job at a place called Ozz - yes it was the place that the wizard came from! This job was to make an airstrip for our fighters. We were laying the metal tracking, which was widely used on the continent. The large area that had been taken over for this purpose included several cottages and of course the occupants of these had long left. I remember we used one of these cottages to have our tea break in, a welcome shelter. The interior was rather ancient, with a large open fireplace. We as usual, had taken advantage of making a fire. The favourite way of doing this was to half fill a tin with petrol, yes, believe it or not, you can do this safely! It should be an open top bucket like tin, once lit it would keep burning until the fuel was all used up. It was this kind of fire that we had in this rather small room which was this time full of lads drinking tea. Everything was alright until some twit threw the remains of his tea mug into the burning petrol. This caused a big bang and a sheet of flame that reached literally across the room. There was no serious injury, but everyone suffered singed hair and eyebrows - another lucky escape.

We were now looking in the direction of Germany, and after the hard fighting around Arnhem the front line was on the move again and this time it was towards the German border. Directly between ourselves and the border, lay Venlo and the river Mass, which we crossed by pontoon, and beyond to Krefeld, where there was a big part of the German industry. We found that we were hot on the heels of the retreating Germans.

It was late in the day when we arrived and we pulled into what was a big boiler works. I well remember stopping after our usual dash forward. It was eleven o'clock at night and dark. We had a big mug of tea and some biscuits (hard tack). Then we all crept into the most comfortable places we could find, for a very much needed rest - but alas - the next thing I knew was someone telling me to get up. We were moving again. It was two o'clock and we had been asleep for three hours. It appeared that our stop was to allow the front troops to capture the airfield that we were to work on. And so, not too far away, we arrived at the airfield - part of it anyway, as it had not been cleared, as I found much to my concern, when the Warrant Officer detailed me to take my machine to the other end of the airfield, but he said 'Wait until that small arms firing stops'!

We were to stay long enough to repair the runways and we were then on the way again. The resistance was now far less effective and our, the allie's advance, speeded up. We were after all actually in Germany and here the Germans had been fairly confident that the fighting would be kept out, consequently the defences were not as well prepared as they had been in other countries. What was most obvious was the damaged caused by the allied bombing over the years and if you consider also the shelling associated with the latest fighting then you will probably realise the vast damage to towns, villages and industry.

It was not long before we were on the move again. We were heading north towards the Baltic Sea and to the west of Berlin. In this area the situation was changing. The gunfire and the resistance was virtually nil, though there were thousands of prisoners. I was a member of a small party travelling in the back of a trooper and I remember we were queuing to cross the river Elbe on the pontoon bridge and we were surrounded by hundreds of British prisoners of war. On this occasion, we ourselves had just been able to get bread - the prisoners saw me in the wagon and I remember one saying, 'Look, there is a real airman,' and they also saw the loaves of bread. I started throwing a loaf or two but I soon realised that there were so many that I threw all the bread. They just broke up the loaves into large pieces and shared them between them.

We crossed the river Elbe and the situation was chaotic with thousands of Germans surrendering together with our prisoners coming out of the prison camp. A little further on progress was now very slow. We came to a point where the German army were all being directed by members of the British Forces onto a large common, where all the vehicles were being parked, German, that is, and the soldiers were being marshalled to another area. Just as we approached, I remember a German military vehicle coming towards us with several SS officers in it. They had by-passed the entrance which they should have entered the field by and the British officer who was directing the traffic shouted us to stop them - this we did with pleasure! The British prisoners were going into the field where the German vehicles were parked and taking some to head for the channel port and home. A few tried to get petrol from us but we were not able to help them.

The Allies advance had now become a route and we were moving north as fast as we could. We were heading in the direction of the Baltic Sea. There were areas that were being passed by the fighting and as we were west of Berlin we were not too far from the Russians who had by now taken Berlin. So we found ourselves greeting some of the first 'friendly' forces. We all embraced each other. We advanced without any signs of resistance, it was more of an obstruction, caused by the German prisoners who were surrendering in droves.

We were now heading toward Lubeck and it was to the airfield as we had always done. but this was completely different. When we entered we were the first British, and indeed, the first allied troops here and as the Germans had now 'finished', everything had been left completely normal - except for the aircraft; all of these had been burned - about a hundred of them.

My memories of the first day at Lubeck was that all the messes, work places, hangars, workshops etc. had been left just as if the people had gone to lunch. I remember towards night time. Aircraft were landing, mostly Germans surrendering. We waited for the few last ones and as we did it was getting dark. I remember someone suggesting providing some lights to guide the aircraft in and the attitude was, 'why should we, its only a German'.

We, the lads, went to explore the various places which were all open to us. The clothing store was absolutely full of clothing, including flying clothing and as we were all trying them on for size, we ended up knee-deep in clothing.

We finished up in the Officers Mess and this like all the other places was well stocked, especially the bar. We were however, very wary as we were always on the look out for poisoned food and drink but somehow or other, we soon got to consuming the contents of the various bottles. Our Warrant Officer (bless him} W. 0. Stone was the one who taught us to test everything and make sure that we were not poisoned. However, here he kept reminding us of the dangers and advising us not to 'overdo it', while he himself got attached to a little spirit measure, drinking as he thought, just a little. But little did he realise that some of us kept filling it up continuously and by the time that we would have been going to bed, he himself had become unable to climb the stairs. He had been standing up all evening and toasting 'here's to the next man to die', so he ended up by being carried to bed himself.

As the fighting had now stopped, we found ourselves wandering around the camp and we found that all the German barrack blocks were all unoccupied and seemed a good place to sleep. We occupied these blocks and it turned out that for some reason the cellars had lots of ammunition for the 'Varey' pistols, the object that the controller fires into the air to signal the aircraft landing. Well, we decided that we had other uses for these. As the barrack blocks faced each other we decided that we would fire the projectiles at each other. Well, just imagine the result. I don't know how, but we were told next morning that a fuel bowser and an aircraft of some kind had been burned out.

All this happened in a very short space of time, and we still had our task of repairing the runways which did have some sabotage damage. As soon as the runway was serviceable there were hundreds of our aircraft landing. There was literally a complete circle of large aircraft completely around the perimeter track which is normally three miles around. These were used to take the prisoners of war back home to France and to the United Kingdom.

CHAPTER VII

VOYAGE TO THE FAR EAST VIA THE PANAMA CANAL

The war on the continent ended on what became known as V.E. Day (Victory in Europe), this was on May 8th, 1945, but although the Germans and its allies had surrendered, the Japanese were still fighting in the Pacific and as a result, we soon found ourselves preparing to go to the 'Far East' to get involved with the Japs. First of all some of us were to return to England for some well earned leave and then to prepare for our journey to the East.

The transportation of troops and equipment in those days was carried out mainly by means of ships and so it was that we were to become the care and maintenance party on several cargo boats, which were to transport all our machines and equipment to the Far East. As the war was still going on out there, we were, we found out eventually, scheduled to go to an island off Okinawa for the invasion of Japan. We found this out later of course, as we were never told of our destination until we were well out to sea. I was, with other of the RAF boys, allocated as a member of the party to voyage on board the 'S S Samdart'. It was a cargo ship, one of the many ships loaned to us by our fellow Americans, one of 'Uncle Sam's Boats' - hence the name Samdart. This was all part of the 'lease lend' arrangement between us and the Americans.

We had sailed out of Liverpool on the 24th July, 1945 to cross the Atlantic bound for America. Our speed on the cargo boat was around 15 knots and we were involved in maintaining the cargo, our plant machines each morning up to lunch time and that in the very warm climate was sufficient, so we had the afternoons free. In this way we crossed the Atlantic in sixteen days, arriving in the bay and anchoring in preparation to sail through the Panama Canal on the 9th August.

We docked in the canal in Colon, this was on the night of the 8th August, and it so happened that this was the day that the Japanese war finished, it was to be known as V.J. Day. This of course meant that our mission to Okinawa was not required. So, when we went ashore, it was to join in the celebrations to mark this very important occasion.

To those that are not familiar with this part of history - the surrender of the Japs was brought about as a result of the dropping, by the Americans, of the first ever 'Atomic' bomb. We had a really good night out in the various clubs, bars and night clubs. It was for me the first time I had experienced this kind of life. We had great fun going in and out of the batwing doors and I remember when we were in one of these establishments, someone threw a cracker-banger through the door.

I should mention here that our ship was only one of seven separate ships, so there was quite a few of us around the pubs that night. I mention this because it involved another of our lot. We were together during the evening and night and after quite a few drinks. I, along with others, helped this person back to the ship on the dock. He was, I may say, feeling rather sick and it so happened that I ended up holding his dentures. After it was all over and I was back on board my ship, I discovered that I still had his dentures in my pocket. We sailed early next morning, so he did not get his dentures back!

The journey through the Panama Canal is an experience that I would not have missed. On the Atlantic end of the canal, the ship enters and leaves three separate locks, each one lifting the ship up to the level of the next high lock by means of the water that is moved from one lock to another. The ship is towed from one to another by means of small locomotives travelling on rails along and parallel to the ship. So, I have said, in my way of looking at it, that the ship literally travelled up-hill. The reason I say this, is that we eventually arrived on a natural lake, looking back down from whence we came. We were now free to travel under our own steam. Conditions on the lake were sub-tropical, with vegetation on either side in which lived many different creatures - like monkeys, parrots, snakes and crocodiles.

We had by now, started to take mepocrin tablets for protection against malaria, these had a tendency to give you a yellowish colour. So with this and the effect of the climate we all looked a bit strange.

The length of the Panama Canal from the Atlantic to the Pacific is around eighty to ninety miles. So, it was not long before we had to think of descending down to the Pacific. This would be by the same method as our entry, by means of locks. The only difference, supposedly is that there is one more lock on the Pacific side, and it seemed that the Atlantic and the Pacific were on different levels! However, we eventually ended up out on the Pacific Ocean and heading for the next port of call, which was to be the Marshall Islands, quite some distance away, in fact half way across the Pacific between America and Singapore. Now, as we were on a cargo boat, the journey was to take us some weeks, but we did not really mind this - working for the first half of the day with the other half free to do what we wanted but not to go where we wanted to! We did play games on board - we played darts, deck quoits, deck tennis etc., and of course there was a lot of lying around in the sun. One thing that I will never forget, it was one day after lunch, I decided to sit on the foremost point of the boat, in other words on the bow. I sat literally with one leg each side of the bows, my back resting against the small derrick boom. I was enjoying myself; watching the shoals of flying fish rising and falling in front of the ships bows, as we dipped and rose against the swell, I was enjoying it that much that I fell asleep and it must have been some considerable time later when I suddenly awoke and realised the danger that I had exposed myself to, I was in a position where I could have fallen off directly in front of the bows and no one would have known about it.

We spent many days, in fact weeks, in the Pacific, day after day the same with no sign of land of any kind. When we had been at sea for nearly four weeks, after leaving the Panama, we saw a small group of islands - this to me was always very mysterious, the questions going through my mind at that time bearing in mind that we had not seen any land for nearly a month, I wondered what was there? Were there any inhabitants, were they watching us? Who knows! But, did I want to know? Maybe not! It would spoil the air of mystery, Then I discovered that these islands were the approaches to the larger group of islands known as the Marshalls. We were to anchor at the island of Eniwetok for the purpose of replenishing our supplies on board, primarily fresh water.

I believe at that time that these islands and the Philippines had been retaken from the Japanese by the American General McArthur and his men and were in fact American Protectorates. We did not stay any longer than was necessary and we were soon on our way once more heading for the Philippines, I think that I should mention here that some of our other ships were also anchored and the poor man that I had helped back in Colon, America, was most pleased to get his dentures back.

This was the twelfth of August and we had it appeared, a fourteen day voyage to Singapore - our ultimate destination, but we would call at the Philippine Islands on our way, Our voyage to these islands was just an extension of what we had already done and we arrived once more near the island of Lete, This was somewhat different to the Marshalls ,it seemed anyway, far more primitive.

We were told, and again as I looked at the island shores, that the head hunters were still active, but what we saw was quite different. The difference was most obvious, in that there were dozens of small boats around the anchorage, going between the anchored ships. It seemed that they were trading their goods of mainly shells, necklaces and bracelets for souvenirs, in return they would get bottles of pop, cigarettes and chocolates. All transactions were carried out by means of a rope lowered over the side of the ship. One such exercise really sticks in my mind - it involved a young Philippino girl that traded in this fashion all day, receiving mainly bottles of pop and lemonade. You can imagine the amount that she would have accumulated in her boat. It happened in the latter part of the day and I happened to be watching when she decided to treat herself to a drink from one of the bottles and when she tasted the contents, it turned out to be water, she was to say the least, disgusted. I realised that probably all the bottles contained water, what a rotten trick, I thought. There were of course, one may guess, other boats with girls in, especially after dark. But what amused me most of all during the day, was the scores of children swimming around - some were really young, possibly only five or six years old. All were engaged in diving for coins, which we threw into the water.

We sailed out of the Philippines on the 23rd September, bound for our final destination - Singapore. We were now well used to the sea. How about saying 'we were seasoned!' So the reminder of our voyage was fairly average. We did, I remember, experience some very rough weather, but not on this section. While we were in the middle of the Pacific, I remember a Yankee ship passing us and as usual it was a lot faster than our little cargo boat. They passed by fairly close to our starboard side and just as they went by I head someone shout, 'Come on your goddamn Limeys', not a very complimentary remark, but when you are in the middle of the ocean, anybody or any other human seems friendly.

CHAPTER VIII

SINGAPORE

We arrived in Singapore harbour on the 26th September. We had of course been re-directed here instead of our original destination Okinawa. So, all the Sam boats carrying our squadron Plant and maintenance crews had either landed or were due to do so soon. This meant that we would all be involved in unloading the plant machines and transport from the ships. During this period we lived aboard the various ships.

When ships are unloaded in the docks, this is carried out by local dockers. Our cargo was mainly very heavy Plant machines and lorries. These would be lifted off by the 50 ton crane, which was part of the ships equipment. On the deck of our ship, we had maybe six to eight lorries, all loaded side by side. When the unloading commenced I remember the crane lifting a heavy bulldozer, dropped the load and it came down across all the lorries and the crane came down as well. In spite of this, unloading went on until some of the holds were emptied. When the larger volume of the hold was empty, it still left the bottom part which was the 'V' shape, down to the keel at the bottom of the boat. Now, this area was filled up with rations, what were known as 'compo' rations. Square cardboard boxes filled with two or three dozen tins of food and various necessities, sufficient for fourteen men for one day, and included in the boxes were sufficient cigarettes for the day. Somehow or other the local stevedores that were unloading these boxes, became aware of the cigarettes and at that time English cigarettes were scarce and much in demand. So, when the cardboard boxes arrived out of the hold, each box had neat hole in one corner in an identical position, just above the tins of cigarettes. Somehow we had to put a stop to this and I was one of the men detailed to guard the cargo, with instructions to shoot at anyone interfering with the contents of the boxes. This did stop the pilfering. We all worked and lived on the ships in the dock until the loads had been cleared. I was just about beginning to realise what life was like in Singapore, living and sleeping on the docks, made us used to the customs and smells around us. For instance; one day I happened to go up one of the side alleys from the actual dock - this was where the dockers ate their midday meal. They all sat in two rows, each side of the alley; some others who brought the food in buckets carried on a pole on their shoulders, each man carried two buckets. They went along sharing the contents out to each individual sitting on the floor. The food consisted of some kind of meal or rice, but mainly fish. I never saw much of it, but oh, what a smell. It was dished out onto big pieces of banana leaves. Needless to say, I did not go up that alleyway again. We were, as I mentioned the care and maintenance party on each boat, caring for the plant and MT during the long voyage from England. There were approximately twenty of us on each boat. What would happen to us now that our job was over? Well, in the last few days, a troop ship had arrived with our complete wing, with hundreds of men. They had left England many weeks after us and had made the voyage in three weeks. So we all formed up together.

There were two main RAF airfields in Singapore. One was RAF Seletar and the other RAF Changi. The latter was well known in association with British prisoners held by the Japanese in Changi jail. I was posted initially to Seletar - it was a pre-war airfield and had been used by the Japanese during their occupation of the island. During our initial time in Singapore the Japanese that had been taken prisoner by the British, were still there in vast numbers. Some of the British Army had the job of looking after these. I remember each day, units could request a certain number of Japanese to work for them. We had them on several occasions - others were kept occupied in many different way. I remember a familiar scene that I saw each day - there were two huge mounds of coal dust which was used for the power house and due to the very hot conditions, these had to be moved to prevent them from really burning up. A gang of Jap prisoners were engaged in transferring the coal dust from one mound to another, using the shallow baskets that they used to carry material around. They would continuously move the dust from one side to the other, until the whole heap was transferred and then move it all back again. I remember one day, some of them were forced to run up and down the roadway, they had obviously done something wrong. I did not really like this, but I suppose that they would have done the same thing with us if they had won the war.

We were soon to be operating our machines as there was a lot to be done, or should I say, undone, as the Japs had really changed the place to defend it against the British. They had constructed large earthen shelters to protect their vehicles and guns. Also underground air-raid shelters. I was involved in levelling these out as there was no real need for them any longer.

We had all now been posted to the new Airfield Construction Squadron, which was 5012 A.C. Squadron. After some time working at Seletar, I along with others were moved to Tengha where we were to build a complete airfield. There was nothing at Tengha, so we were back to living in tents again, with primitive facilities, like toilets which were just holes dug in the ground and wooden boxes with holes in to sit on and the whole lot was surrounded by hessian. We used nick-names for the actual toilets, we called them thunder boxes. I will remember for a long time to come my experience on one of these. After using one, having spent considerable time, I was adjusting my dress and I was facing the 'thunder box' I was horrified to see a huge scorpion crawl out from inside of the wooden seat. Had I sat there a little longer I would have come to grief!

Our work at Tengah entailed moving a very large hill, or I suppose you could say, a little mountain. However, the idea was to bring the hill down into the valley, so that we could have a large flat area. There would be dozens of bulldozers and scrapers all crawling over the hill, just like ants, filling from the top of the hill and bringing it down into the valley. Operating these big diesel machines in the hot sun was not easy. We wore hardly any clothing, my memory is of seeing one operator standing on the deck of his machine, in his birthday suit, maybe not exactly, as the metal on the machine was so hot that you had to have shoes or otherwise you would burn your feet.

Thinking back to my work in Singapore, while at Seletar, I worked on a vehicle earthen shelter on the road near the officers mess. Like the others that I worked on, the idea was to reshape the soil to make it as flat as possible, but leaving the middle, so that when it was finished, it looked something like a cove. I was in fact changing the face of the land. Some years later when I returned to Seletar, in Singapore, I revisited the area where I had worked, nothing had changed, it was all still the same shape.

CHAPTER IX

RETURN VOYAGE

As the war had been over for some time, there was a scheme for releasing some of the members of the forces that had joined up for what was known as 'the duration of the present emergency' and now that the emergency was over, the release would begin. There was a system of numbers (group numbers) arrived at by age and length of service, and accordingly your date of release. My group was in September, 1946, but there would be leave included in this and it brought my actual date to the 9th July, 1946. As we had originally been going for the invasion of Japan and had been diverted to Singapore, our tour was not a regular one. So we were to return to the UK in April.

Our return trip was the opposite way to our voyage out to Singapore. We came through the Indian Ocean, Red Sea, Gulf of Aden, Suez Canal, Mediterranean, Gibraltar, Bay of Biscay, Atlantic Ocean to Southampton. The voyage was on a troop ship, the 'Capetown Castle'. It took just twenty days - the record was at that time, nineteen days. This was held by a ship called The Andes. We arrived in Southampton and we were welcomed by a military band. I had now travelled by ship completely around the world through both the Panama and Suez Canals.

So the war was over, the present emergency was also over - come to think of it this was the emergency that I had joined the RAF for. All the men that were regulars, in other words those that had joined up before the war, for a specified number of years would remain in and continue until the end of their contract. The rest of us would leave. My thoughts went back now to the time when I joined and all the efforts that I made to get into the RAF but now, due to everyone else feeling they wanted to get out as soon as possible, I suppose I was going along with the tide. The other factor, and probably the most

impressionable for me was that my mother was looking forward to my coming out of the RAF and back home again.
The question that I asked asked myself, was it what I wanted? Would I be undoing the dream that I had had for half my life? Was that it? Before I joined up I would ask myself - am I in the right place, job etc.? But I thought that if I joined the RAF whether it was right or not, I would have to serve and that is what I really wanted - having to serve. Now that I was to lose this security, I really did not like it. But for the time being this was it and we all went on leave to return for the last time to be demobbed.

There were thousand of military personnel to be demobbed, so a demob centre had been set up to deal with this. Every serviceman was entitled to a fair deal. So, towards this, we were all issued with a complete civilian rigout, from suit to underclothes. Then there was the long two or three months leave, with pay. Some took advantage of the resettlement courses and indeed some even went in for longer periods of study. The demob centre was at Cardington, if I remember. So, this is where I finally left the RAF.

SECTION 111

CHAPTER X

CIVILIAN LIFE

I was therefore to become a civilian, after four and three quarter years service. My immediate outlook was, I must admit, a little naive because I was prepared to live out my long leave and not think of finding a job. It was not until my mother mentioned the fact that I could be working. What was I going to do? After the trouble I had experienced in freeing myself from the clutches of the C.W.A.E.C. (Country War Agricultural Executive Committee) I did not even think of going back to that kind of work. I had been trained to operate a variety of construction plant equipment in the RAF. But this had not spread to my part of the country yet. My other attribute, was of course, the use of a variety of tools to carry out manual work.

My brother Ben had spent the majority of his life working for the council so this was a thought, as most people thought that a job with the council was a job for life. I eventually investigated the possibility and believe it or not I was offered a job of looking after the county council roads in Llangynog - on my doorstep really.

At that time the county council employed lengthmen - that was men who looked after a given length of road, this would be about twenty miles. He would normally be his own boss, to work where he chose and to carry out what work he thought was necessary. The only direct connection with the council was a foreman with a roving commission, who would put in an appearance once or twice a month.

I was initially assigned to a regular lengthman, who had for some short time, worked on a 'length'. So together we would carry out the variety of work on that particular length. It was still summer and the work was quite pleasant, out in the open air all day. The hours were from 07.30 to 16.30 with fifteen minutes for morning break and thirty minutes for lunch, which comprised of sandwiches that I brought with me every day, and tea from a thermos flask. The lengthman that I was to work with was a man by the name of Wat Cole. He lived in a village about three or four miles from my home. I thought that Wat was a friendly person, aged about fifty, very talkative and fun to be with - but his ability as a lengthman left a lot to be desired. I found this out in a very short time. I had the valuable experience of this kind of work, as it was similar to farm work. Maybe it will be necessary for me to explain that all the work, like hedge trimming and verge cutting, was done manually with a scythe and sickle and to carry out this work successfully you needed very sharp tools, so, like the snooker player chalks his cue, you are regularly re-sharpening your tools. It was very obvious from the work that Wat did, that he hardly every sharpened his sickle - the result was that instead of cutting the trash cleanly and neatly he kind of 'hit it to death' - yes you could see some actually come out by the roots. The other memorable thing was Wat Cole, a bit unkind maybe, was, when we sat down for our sandwiches, he had the most peculiar habit of stuffing his mouthfull, then kept feeding in more. He reminded me very much of a little hamster, with his cheeks puffed out. But of course table manners were not really as important out in the middle of nowhere, except for the occasional robin or blackbird that sometimes came around for crumbs.

After a month or two with Wat Cole, I was moved to a neighbouring 'length' to assist another lengthman by the name of Ted Protheroe. Ted had not been a lengthman very long. In those days a lengthman's job was considered to be a prestigious one. Each length when compared was different; therefore some were preferred to others. The locality where we worked was all in Llangynog, and very much country. There were very few villages and, as the farms were situated away from the roadside, some stretches were really lonely. The traffic consisted of the occasional car, tradesmen's vans, the odd bicycle and a few pedestrians, some of which would stop to have a chat. Depending on the area or part of your length that you would be working on, you would see some 'regulars'.

I remember one old lady that travelled the road everyday, except maybe weekends. She would walk the two miles to the main road to catch a bus to Carmarthen to collect a few groceries apparently. This daily trip was necessary as her husband would only trust her with limited amounts of money each day. She was a very 'simple' person. I remember one day she stopped to talk to me as usual and she was asking me for my opinion on the shoes that she was wearing. These were, I discovered, men's shoes - her husbands and were at least two sizes too large. Her husband apparently was not very kind to her, but they got along somehow.

After a short period of time working with Ted, I was at last given my own length. My predecessor here was an elderly man by the name of Johnny 'Humberton'. Humberton was not really his surname, it came from the place that he used to live in. This is typical of the Welsh way of referring to people either by their home, house, or even job. I think he had worked on this length for the majority of his working life and was now due to retire and I was therefore his replacement.

All the roads around this area were all small country ones, some were used solely by farmers. I worked on some roads that were very lonely - in fact I could go to work in some places, in the morning and not see a soul all day. Such a road was 'Cwm Cremlin' - huh, in those days I did not associate this name with a place in Russia. Come to think of it though, a strange name for a Welsh location. This was without a doubt, the most desolate spot around. When I worked in places like this, I sometime thought back to my RAF days, not for the similarity but for the contrast. I still had this RAF feeling - I could not really settle, but two things kept me on the road. One was the fact that I could always take pride in whatever job I did and to this end I

ELIM

As you travel through the valley
Between its densely wooded sides,
You'll come to a little clearing –
Not really very wide.

There, standing in the corner,
Neatly tucked away,
Stands a little Chapel
Where people go to pray.

Facing all the sunshine
Protected from the gales
You'll find little Elim Chapel,
In the valley down in Wales.

There's a little rustic bridge
That crosses o'er the brook
Where the cool clear water babbles
As in the ' Shady Nook'.

Elim stands there in the corner
Watching o'er the dead
Under rows and rows of tombstones,
One at every head.

There is one that's very special,
Special as you will see.
It's marked 'Tom and Margaret Lewis"
But mum and dad to me.

worked to achieve the best results. The other reason was of course the same one that brought me out of the RAF - my mother (God bless her). She did her best in her simple way to try and make me comfortable at home from my lonely job. I did find some relief by my visits to the village 'local', where we played darts etc. This was about a mile away. I probably visited the pub fairly frequently - too frequent for my mum, but I used the excuse that I was going for a packet of cigarettes. My mum though on odd occasions would produce a packet from her apron pocket, in spite of the fact that she was very much against the smoking habit. So, I could not really leave home to rejoin the RAF while my mother was there. I continued my work on the road and there were times when I would work nearer the main road and civilisation. I would on these occasions, see people passing to and fro and being a road man you get to know most people. I had on several occasions spoken to a door-to-door salesman - if that is what you call a man who makes pegs and sells them! He was apparently an ex Royal Marine and a very smart one at that. He married one of the local girls and when he was demobbed he went back to selling pegs. You may wonder what that has got to do with my story, well, one day when I was ditching along the roadside, he came and talked about his days in the Marines and mine in the RAF. While we were talking he referred to me and my job - he said that I was in a rut, and at that time I had one foot in the ditch! He was of course referring to my sticking it out on the road, when I really wanted to rejoin the RAF. Well, he made me think.

I had now been out of the RAF for well over a year and had been reasonably contented but now I was once more thinking about the RAF as I did in the old days, but this time with some knowledge and experience. It was now 1947, and if that year was noted for anything, it has to do with the 'big freeze up' - it was March and we awoke one morning to see the heaviest snowfall of all time. I have seen nothing to compare with it before or since. So many things happened then that it would make a story of its own, but if I can briefly describe the conditions; the snow had fallen overnight and when we tried to look out we could not see through the windows. Situated where we were it was difficult to assess the situation. We could move around outside, with difficulty, to tend the animals and milk father's cows. Then we tried to do the normal thing, take the churns to the milkstand - about a quarter of a mile away - from where it would normally be collected by lorry. Although we did get there, it would have been there for a very long time as it was impossible for any vehicle to travel on the road. I have vivid memories of that very difficult morning, very cold and freezing and we normally used wood for our fire, this was now buried under several feet of snow. There was no other means of cooking or heating so to have a cup of tea you had to light a fire. I cannot remember whether or not we had a radio at that time, so I cannot say whether there was any news of the weather. What I do remember is that at that time my mother was not very well, she had been in bed for some time and on this particular morning required a doctor or something from him. Now, there was no phone in our house or anywhere near, even if there had been one, the lines were all down. That was electric and telephone. So the only way to the doctor was by 'shank's pony'. Yes you guessed it - walking.

If I remember correctly I started out on the journey with a bike, thinking that if had to carry it over the snow on the minor roads, I could probably ride it on the main road. The main problem, I think now, was that accompanying the heavy snow was a fierce gale and the effect of this was that in certain clear areas and in other places there were drifts ten feet high and in some places much higher. I was still on the minor road making slow progress towards the main road, and as these country roads do turn and twist in different directions I came to a spot where the wind was blowing directly across the road. Consequently the snow had started building up on one side of the road gradually built up across the road, until it had nearly reached the other side at about a height of fifteen feet. To get past this I would have to get through the tunnel that was left; I tried this but after a very short distance I had to retreat as the fine snow that was being swirled around by the wind prevented me from breathing. I eventually had to go off the road and walk through the field until I finally reached the main road, only to find that there was not much difference, it too was covered in deep snow and high drifts. I still had my bike believe it or not; I had carried it so far but it looked as if it was all in vain. As I went along towards St Clears, I came to a hill which faced the wind and the effect was that there were two clear areas with a terrific high bank of snow in the middle of the road. I had my bike and I was blown effortlessly up the hill. At the top I was back to deep snow - to cut a long story short, I got there and saw the doctor, and returned home with similar troubles, especially on the hill which I just mentioned, where I was blown upwards, I now could not ride down against the wind and as I was now going in the opposite direction I was on the wrong side of the drift, so when I came to the bottom of the hill I was faced with a dead end surrounded by high walls of snow, so, I had to go back to the top again, around the end of the drift and down the other side. I eventually reached home, tired, hungry and soaking wet. I cannot remember what I had brought but I know that it was really 'required'. That was the kind of journey that one could not forget, so, as I write this I have relived it all again.

The big freeze up, as it became known, disrupted everything and it was some time before communication was established as the snow was to remain for weeks. Now as a lengthman, responsible for many miles of lonely road, you can possible realise the importance of clearing these roads, so that people could get the services and the necessities of ordinary living.

There could be no question of using machines to clear the snow, as it would not be possible with such depths. So, it befell volunteers to do so by hand. I could recruit any person and as many as necessary. So, each day they would report to me so that I could record their time and they would be paid accordingly. I remember, in the deepest places, the drifts were so high that when we stood on the surface, we were level with the top of the telegraph poles.

Time went by; my mother had not been well for some time and now she gradually worsened and I had something else to think about. I had, for as long as I could remember, dreaded the time when I would lose my mother. This is exactly what happened on the 27th December, 1947. I did not think that I would get over it but as we all know, we do. So now, what was to happen to me? I had lost my mum, I was not married but father was still at home and my sister Mary, who at that time had separated from her husband. So, I still had a home with father, Mary and her two children Spencer and Gwennie who were quite young.

I continued to work on the road, but the longer I was in the job, the more I thought that it was not really what I should be doing. I was now thirty years old and for that age, I suppose that I had been around the world and I still thought that there must be somewhere better for me to be.

So, now what was to happen to me? The old feeling, the RAF was still strong, stronger in fact. So, I had again to make a decision regarding my future. For me at that time, a difficult decision – not too easy to solve. In the past my consideration would have been – 'what would mother say'? Now with hindsight, I realised this feeling remained with me for quite some time to come.

I wrote for details of a regular career in the RAF and after a short time received a letter that was to change my life once more. My father was the only thought I had to consider and he had not shown as much concern as my mother had when I left before. So, after considering all the possibilities I decided that I would return to the sanctuary of the RAF which I had longed for, for so long. Although I had achieved my ambition then, it seemed that I had been cheated whan I was released.

I had by now some experience of the two occupations that were to form the greatest part of my life – namely my childhood ambition, farming and my previous RAF experience. I was therefore in an ideal situation to decide my future, although my first love was and always will be, farming, especially in my native Wales. The experience that I had gained in the RAF, had if anything strengthened my preference and as then in the 'tug-of-war', opted for a career in the RAF.

SECTION 1V

CHAPTER X1

RE-ENLISTMENT

I rejoined the RAF on the fourth of January, 1949. I reported to the recruiting unit and although I had been 'out' for some time I was surprised to find that I was to rejoin my old unit that I had left in Germany at the end of the war in 1945.

GERMANY 1950 – On my arrival in Germany I was soon to realize that the role had of course, changed from the war torn destructive 'state' to what appeared to be the new constructive peacetime 'state'. During my years in Germany, we were to construct several complete airfileds, mostly in the south. We were involved in RAF Wildenrath, Bruggen, Geilenkirchen and Goch. These were all constructed around the same period. I spent about three years at, what later became known as RAF Wildenrath. It was very hard and difficult work.

We employed a workforce of several hundred German workers. These were known as GCLO – German Civil Labour Organisation. The force consisted of men from all over Germany, mostly displaced and still affected by the war or the aftermath. There were mixtures of people from north to south and existed as a kind of national mobile workforce.

We were located in the midst of a forest of trees, although part had been cleared for the construction of the airfield, our accommodation was in the middle of the forest. We worked for two and a half years on shift work, from 03.30hrs in the morning to 21.00hrs in the evening. As we were in a densely wooded area, wild life was in abundance. It was where the dawn chorus sounded more like the ' Last Night of the Proms', especially at 3.30am!

Most of my time in Germany was spent on the new airfields under construction, ending at RAF Bruggen in 1954.
Note - I was saddened recently, now, after nearly fifty years, these airfields ceased to be used by the British Airforce.

These years in Germany were eventful ones for me personally. I was promoted several times – ending up in the rank of Warrant Officer.

In 1952 my father passed away and this was a milestone in my life. I had now lost my mother and my father and was seemingly alone – not yet married. Rather a strange thing to say amongst all my RAF colleagues? Maybe. After several years in Germany I returned to the UK.

It was now 1954 and I had been in Germany longer than the stipulated two and and a half years, which was the normal tour period. The reason for this was that I had been involved in the construction of the new airfields and it seemed that my services were appreciated to the extent that I was asked to remain until the projects were completed.

RETURN TO UK.

RAF Wellesbourne Mounford

While I had been in Germany the successive promotion to Warrant Officer had to say the least, been busy years for me. My promotion had been so accelerated that I had very little time to enable me to become familiar with each new situation. It was what I termed as being 'in at the deep end'. Well, here I was again, in the same situation, only this time in a training environment that was completely new to me. Not only was I in a new situation, I was in charge of a training school with many experienced instructors – it seemed mighty deep!

The training school was near Warwick in the Midlands and it turned out that there were at least some compensations. I met Mollie, a girl from Oakham in Rutland. We became very good friends – so good that as a result we were married in 1956 in Stratford on Avon. I remained at Wellesbourne for a further period during which time our daughter Michelle was born at the Monroe Devis maternity home in Tiddington, just outside Stratford. I was to stay in the UK for a total of seven years before I was once more due for an overseas posting.

CYPRUS AND FAR EAST

My overseas posting soon came and now as a married man, I would have what was known as an accompanied tour. We as a family were posted to RAF Akrotiri in Cyprus. After about a year it seemed that our services were needed far more in the East and we were moved to Singapore. From there we were to service an area of a thousand miles eastwards to Sarawak and beyond to the island of Labuan in North Borneo and another thousand miles northwards from Singapore to Thailand, where incidentally I was to spend several months of my tour. During the time that we were to serve in these outlandish places our families would of course remain in Singapore.

As I would be responsible for deploying the airmen to these various outposts, I was not to be left out. As an RAF Warrant Officer I was to be in charge of a consignment of RAF personnel and associated equipment, destined to join other military units in Thailand. While I do not intend to relate all my experiences in this brief account, I feel that there may be some worthy of mention.

THE JOURNEY

We sailed out of Singapore on board the 'Empire Kittiwake', a cargo boat that was to take all our heavy equipment to Bangkok in Thailand.

We sailed along the Malaysian coastline to our destination. From there we were to make an overland journey of approximately six hundred miles to a place called Mukdahan.

After disembarking in Bangkok harbour, all the men and materials had to be organised to form a heavy convoy of vehicles to travel overland for the rest of our journey. This entailed a lot of hard work and the men worked up to midnight and, as we were scheduled to start our journey at 4.00am, this left very little time for sleep. I discovered that sleep was in fact far from what the men were thinking of. They were soon to sample the notorious night life of Bangkok. Imagine the problem next morning, trying to 'arouse' the drivers in time to start the journey – (there were no breathalyser tests for what they were suffering from)! All I can say is – that we were late!

The overland journey that we were to make would be in two stages with a break at the American Camp at Korat. It turned out to be long, arduous and eventful, mostly over very rough, rugged and in places seemed 'uncharted territory', most of the way over sand tracks that became deeply rutted. There were many bridges with bridge weight limits which were in most cases exceeded and completely disregarded.

We eventually arrived at our first destination having covered three hundred miles. The drivers having driven, with very little rest, valued and eagerly accepted the hospitality that we were offered and I suppose had come to expect from the Americans – even abroad. We were to spend several days here to re-charge our systems in preparation for the second three hundred miles.

We started the final part of our journey heading for our ultimate destination – Mukdahan. We started with a little better knowledge of the journey ahead and of course with the benefit of experience of the first half. The country and terrain were similar to the past but we

My convoy en route for Ban Phai

Crawler tractors working with scrapers in the latterite dust in Thailand

had a considerable distance when we travelled on a good road, which was referred to as 'The American Highway' only later to revert to a far more basic kind of road with ridges that seemed like a corrugated roof and covered all over with an inch of dust, which resulted in each vehicle following the cloud of dust in front. This made control, from my point of view, very difficult. Bridges and weights remained as inadequate as ever. All had to be negotiated one vehicle at a time. We eventually reached our destination three weeks after leaving Singapore and in spite of all that had happened we managed to arrive with all the vehicles in the convoy.

THAILAND

We had come to Thailand to join other military units. Mainly the British Army, to construct an airfield. I therefore soon discovered that as an RAF Warrant Officer I would be attached to the army and to all intents and purposes be part of an army unit. As one of three Warrant Officers I was senior and as such consequently landed a fair amount of the appropriate resposibilities, including a hundred machine operators that consisted of - British Army, RAF, New Zealand and Australia military - a real mixture.

The work on the airfield was carried out under very difficult conditions as the climate to say the least was hot, the hours were long and due to the continuous work of the plant machines, the dust that was latterite dust, was present during the whole operation. We were accommodated in tents. There were no permanent buildings and we were in the midst of open country, where services of all kinds were basic or non existent. As a result many of the men suffered from various ailments. Some self inflicted, like the one I can refer to and caused by ' maidenly' associations. I escaped for most of the time but eventually fell victim to the dreaded lurgi – enteritis. That can be most troublesome even under normal conditions but out in the wilds of Thailand, most difficult. I mentioned that the services were basic, but just to mention one – the bottom service – in other words, the latrines. While it was hygienic and certainly adequate, it was very basic. It consisted of a series of deep holes in the ground, directly under a long horizontal pole, on which we sat or 'perched' but however basic and uncomfortable, very welcome for me in my urgent state as the enteritis kept me mobile between the tent and the perch. I did recover before the end of my stay but when I eventually returned to Singapore, I had lost a stone in weight and as a bonus I developed shingles. I had by then returned to my wife after an absence of over three months.

My work and effort in Thailand must have been recognised somewhere as I was rewarded by being presented to the AOC (Air Officer Commanding) on the occasion of his annual inspection of our unit later in Singapore.

FINAL RETURN TO THE UK

In nineteen sixty five I returned to the U.K. once more and as it turned out for the last time as a serviceman. I returned to the training school but during my time away it had moved from Warwickshire to Waterbeach in Cambridgeshire. This is where our second daughter Mandy, was born in Ely Hospital, which was then an RAF Hospital but now I believe a NHS Hospital. I had been in the RAF many years and consequently approaching the time when I would complete my twenty two years pensionable service. I applied to be released from the RAF under the special conditions that existed at that time and I was finally released from the RAF in October, 1966. It seemed to be a very opportune time as the government were setting up a major training scheme for all industries, including the construction industry. This was an ideal opportunity for me to continue in the world of training and of course, in the work that had now become my life but in Norfolk - a long way from Wales.

The Annual Ceremonial March Past Air Officer Commanding. Me second from left.

Receiving my Long Service and Good Conduct Medal from the Commanding Officer

SECTION V

CHAPTER X11

THE CONSTRUCTION INDUSTRY BOARD

When I applied to join the CITB (The Construction Industry Training Board) I was applying to the head of the Plant Training Department who was in fact the same head of department that I had in the RAF. So, as we were old aquantances I was accepted without even an interview and I joined the staff of the company in January, 1967. The post that I had applied for was that of an instructor. My job would be to instruct trainees in the driving/operating of the many various types of machines used in the construction indusrtry. This was of course a step down from the position that I had held in the RAF for the past thirteen years as a supervisor but I looked at it as one step down to go up two.

I had, strangely enough, reached the top of my grade in the training world in the RAF and there was no reason why I should not do just as well in a new job. Firstly I enjoyed my job as an instructor and secondly I was working with several of my old associates, some that had worked for me as instructors in the RAF. The work was strenuous in that it involved demonstrating the machines and teaching the trainees in the vast open training areas. There was some classroom instruction involved but most of the time was spent outside in all weathers.

Bircham Newton, as it became known was soon established as a training centre and it grew in strength and reputaion very rapidly as the number of trained men attended the courses and returned to the industry to spread the gospel of training.

After a relatively short period in my position as instructor, my potential as an organiser became 'apparent or so it seemed, as my boss recommended that I should be promoted to supervisor but as the CITB organisation had not long been established there was no such position. The department where I worked, had like everything else, grown in size. There were approximately twenty instructors so there was a requirement for supervision. To this end my boss used me in the position of senior instructor – the situation was theoretical and unpaid. I had then to supervise instructors that I had been working alongside in the previous week. So once more I was finding my level as I had done in my previous jobs. My position was soon ratified and I officially became the first senior instructor. Eventually I found myself in charge of the whole of the plant training department, including responsibility for making recommendations regarding the purchase of new equipment with a very generous budget.

As a senior instructor I travelled to various companies and countries. I was also involved in the annual exhibition of construction plant - Site Equipment Demonstration - that was held in Hatfield where I was asked to judge the performance of operators and select a winner each year. The reason for my involvement was that Bircham Newton Training Centre was supposed to be the correct source of safe operating – so who better to judge than the senior instructor - Plant Training. I did this for ten years.

Bircham Newton had now developed into a centre for the training of all construction trades and by 1969/70 the Civil Engineering College for young boys from the age of seventeen – near enough school leaving age – was formed. Originally there were two hundred boys, each sponsored by a construction company. Later the number of boys increased and we in the plant department had one hundred boys. This I found very interesting, although at times it was very trying but most would settle down amongst the others with the right persuasion. The programme of training included periods of time when the boys would complete projects away from the centre – mostly local. One such venue was a very well known estate, The Royal Estate at Sandringham.

As the year went by the training centre became more well known for the kind of training carried out there and probably most of all it was the safety aspect that attracted the most attention, due to the attrocious safety record of the construction industry with its many deaths during the years.

I think that I should mention the time when our working site became a venue for a TV film that was made at the centre by the Goodies – Graham Garden , Bill Oddie and Tim Brook-Taylor, the TV trio. The reason for coming to our site was that they would use our plant machines as part of their comedy film – that turned out to be very funny. The filming took place during a time that did not interrupt the training programme.

We would, like most organisations be visited by various dignitaries, who were invited to come and see the work that we did for the industry. These would range from local officials to government ministers. During these occasions it was my job to take these people on the plant equipment where they would receive a sample of the instruction – this was also good for our publicity. I would be photographed alongside these people who included – the Minister of Eployment. I remember Sir Geoffrey Howe who later became deputy Prime Minister, Lord Carr and several others. The most important of all I suppose was His Royal Highness The Duke of Edinborough – Prince Phillip. This was of course the ultimate, every one after that was just common!

Due to our close proximity to the Royal residence at Sandringham, we got involved through the training with the staff on the estate. Before I retired, during my final year at the training centre, we, (me,

my wife and two daughters) had an invitation to a Royal Garden Party at Buckingham Palace.

I had by now completed many years at the Centre and I had, as before, reached the position and place in the management that was to be my level. I finally retired in nineteen eighty three and due to my family ties I have remained here in Norfolk, still a long way from my homeland.

SIR GEOFFREY HOWE AND ME

PRINCE PHILIP AND ME

FOSTERING

In the nineteen seventies we became foster parents to children in need of a place of refuge. In order to qualify as foster parents, it was necessary to be vetted by Social Services. This vetting was quite exhaustive and entailed a lot of enquires by them. After some considerable time we were accepted by them and became foster parents for several years.

For some time previous to our commitment, we, specially my wife, Mollie, was of the opinion that she would like to get involved in helping children in need of love and friendship and to this end we had visions of the young children involved. However, things are not always as they seem and now having been involved I can relate from experience and it is from experience that I relate, not in any way as an authority on the subject.

Children in need are so, simply because of the circumstances within the family home and invariably this is to do with the parents - it could be of course, the lack of parents. So in most cases the children in need of care, the ones that we are most likely to encounter would be to say the least, disturbed, difficult and probably in need of care and affection. They are further disturbed by the fact that they are removed from their familiar surroundings and placed in a strange home with people they do no know.

We served as short term Foster Parents for those children that had to be taken from their homes in an emergency and placed in a secure refuge. So fostering is not as simple as it seems at first. All the lovely, happy, little children that we see around, are happy and do not need fostering. But with hindsight, in the end, fostering can be very rewarding and satisfying and we are pleased to have been involved.

RETIREMENT

Many people that I have spoken to have looked forward to retirement, to be free. A lot of these have still been of the same opinion after retirement but are surprised by the sudden change – loss of pressure etc. I have now been retired for over seven years and feel that I am qualified to remark on the subject at least as far as it has affected me. When the final day of work came, the last day on which I was to leave, to be quite honest I was sorry but to be like most people I think that I must have pretended that I was pleased. I think really, looking back at it now, when we are at work we look forward to a holiday but when that holiday becomes the norm, we then look forward to work.

I have just finished writing the story of my Life's Work and anyone reading it would agree that I was a workaholic. It was my life, it was my pleasure. If one is involved in ones own business, work and life just go on and is not normally interrupted by retirement. If you are in employment, that day when you reach the age of retirement, it is final, but I think that due to my outlook on life, in that I have said that I intend to live to be one hundred years old, this does at least serve as a basis for another phase in my life! So it is the end of the beginning and not the beginning of the end.

I have returned many times to my old place and have had many discussions with people still in employment the question 'what does it feel like to be retired'? One of my famous expressions is 'that it feels like when I was a little boy, you got up on a nice summers morning and thought - what shall I play today'? In other words, freedom to do what you want to do and then you think of doing all those things that you said you were going to do when you retired. But somehow it is not the same, as you are about twenty years older and not always as able. I have however, been trapped between this condition and making a real effort to keep as fit as possible. I do this by having regular habits which I must perform every day. I somehow apply pressure on myself, I feel that I cannot ease off from this as if I did I would be cheating myself. I have regular physical exercises that I do each day, which I think are very important. I am reminded of a remark by one of my golfing colleagues, he said that when he retired, he would have a shave every morning and a drink every night when he finished work. All these things are only possible of course, if you are granted good health. This is taken for granted of course when you are young but it is not so when you are in this part of life.

Most people, when they retire look for leisure, for these it is a fairly simple decision but there are many, like myself, that have thrived on work and find it difficult to exist without it. So, what do we do? I have to keep involved and since my retirement I have a lot of real enjoyment from working with wood. I first got interested in wood when we had woodwork classes in school, but for most of my life I have not had the opportunity to get involved,

My colleagues were trying to decide what to present me with as a leaving present. They asked Mollie my wife and unknown to me Mollie told them of my childhood interest and consequently I was given quite a few woodworking tools. So, gradually I started messing around and before long I discovered that I had a talent and I made my first oak clock case. It was a decorative clock and somehow I managed to copy most of the work from another old clock, so really it was a reproduction, it was very well made and just as good as the original, so most people said, In fact when I took it to an antique specialist his comments were 'It was German, from 1913 and the only thing that had happened to it was that someone had revarnished it. So he could not distinguish my work from the original! So this was the beginning - most important though, it took some time to complete and during the whole of this time I was very involved and completely immersed in the job.

After I had completed this very enjoyable job, I did not continue in this line. So, after these many weeks of involvement there was a kind of anti-climax and I was back to the old feeling of not being involved. Now, Mollie, who has been my inspiration so many times, suggested that I attempt to make another clock, this time a bigger job, a long case clock. At first I did not think that it was even a possibility but with all the spare time I somehow saw that it was possible and I seriously thought of copying the old long case clock that I was given when I was still a school boy, So, I began to plan how I would go about it. I decided eventually, that if I was to do it I would try and make the most difficult pieces first. So, if I was to fail, then I would fail before I had done most of the work. Now I started measuring, sketching and most important, looking. Important, as I have to see the finished product in my mind before I can copy it. I then spent a long time taking measurements and taking these down on paper. This was necessary in order to estimate how much wood I would need. I had already decided that it was to be mahogany and I realised that this was going to be expensive. Eventually, after a lot of enquiries and searching, I found a firm of cabinet makers and I presented them with a list of the various sizes of wood that I required. I had by the way 'drawn' a scale plan - note my drawn in italics - that is in order to emphasize it. I could not really compare it with any other as this is something that I am not good at. I managed a complete list of pieces of wood that I would require and I was told that it would cost about one hundred pounds. So you can imagine, now that I had the wood in the shed, I could start in earnest. I decided to make each part and leave it until had completed all the pieces, then I would fit them all together. Now, if you remember, I enjoyed my first little clock, this project though was to take a whole year. It was the most interesting job that I have ever done. Throughout the whole time that I was involved, I was governed by the fact that I had just sufficient to complete the job - that meant that I could not afford any mistakes, fortunately there were none. Putting it all together was an exciting time as there was no guarantee that all the pieces would match up.

When it was finished I was very proud of the job and it has provided hours of pleasure, simply by looking at it and with hindsight, I cannot believe that I actually made it. Once more - gradually, I felt that the pressure had gone and I had the old feeling of being 'spare', but somehow, from day to day, there is always something that requires doing, especially when you have a large garden. There is in fact so much to do that one wonders how I did manage to do all this while I was still at work.

There is one activity that I have been involved in, even before I retired, and that is golf. I have played regularly, more than once a week. It is a demanding game and requires a fair amount of energy and fitness and like everything else that I do I treat it seriously, maybe for a game, too seriously. I have for some years been a member of the Veterans Section of the local Golf Club. We play together every Tuesday and we get involved in competitions both at home and in several other golf clubs around Norfolk. Mollie had also got involved in the game and we sometimes play together, especially as she has also retired.

I have discovered that with regards to my golf, that the kind of work that I do previously has a marked effect on the standard of play, so I do try to leave the heavier jobs, not too close to my important golf games, but of course we must get our priorities right! I have discovered that above all, it is necessary to exercise the body sufficiently to allow for the function that it is to perform In other words, the body will produce the energy that is necessary if it is treated properly. I have often compared life with riding a bicycle - it is necessary to keep pedalling at all times in order to keep going - there are times when we come to hills, when we must pedal even harder to keep going. Then come the easier times which is like free wheeling down the hill but if we take life too easy, then we keep going down the hill and we will find it hard going to go up the other side. So, in actual life, one must keep the pressure on at all times. I find myself putting on the pressure

most of the day and I therefore really appreciate the welcome relief in the evenings.

Note:-

It is now several years since I penned my last remarks on retirement. Although I may be a little older, the aim or target remains the same, a little bit more difficult to follow maybe as we travel ever onwards.

MEMORY LANE

Today I tried to travel
Down the road to yesteryear,
To see those distant places
That I have always held so dear.

Places like my birthplace,
Places, where as a boy I played,
The school that I attended
And all those friends I'd made.

I saw the old school still standing
Though it educates no more.
The playground now is empty
But I hear voices from before.

I saw the house that we once lived in
And, as I stood there at the gate
I tried to see it as I knew it,
But of course, it was too late.

The roof showed signs of fire
That had happened long ago.
Trees grew in amongst it,
Trees, I did not know.

The walls were still standing,
The windows now just spaces.
When I tried to see inside
I saw just phantom faces.

It was not the gate that I was standing at,
Nor the walls of that old shrine
That prevented me from entering,
It was the invisible wall of time.

Time has claimed so many things
But many still remain.
How I loved that special journey
Amongst those things again.

As we travel down life's highway,
All the lanes go just one way
Except maybe, one called memory –
The one I went down today.

THE END

BIRCHAM NEWTON
TRAINING CENTRE.